No More Low Expectations for English Learners

Dear Readers,

Much like the diet phenomenon *Eat This, Not That*, this series aims to replace some existing practices with approaches that are more effective—healthier, if you will—for our students. We hope to draw attention to practices that have little support in research or professional wisdom and offer alternatives that have greater support. Each text is collaboratively written by authors representing research and practice. Section 1 offers a practitioner's perspective on a practice in need of replacing and helps us understand the challenges, temptations, and misunderstandings that have led us to this ineffective approach. Section 2 provides a researcher's perspective on the lack of research to support the ineffective practice(s) and reviews research supporting better approaches. In Section 3, the author representing a practitioner's perspective gives detailed descriptions of how to implement these better practices. By the end of each book, you will understand both what not to do, and what to do, to improve student learning.

It takes courage to question one's own practice—to shift away from what you may have seen throughout your years in education and toward something new that you may have seen few if any colleagues use. We applaud you for demonstrating that courage and wish you the very best in your journey from this to that.

Best wishes,

— *Nell K. Duke and Ellin Oliver Keene, series editors*

No More
Low Expectations
for English
Learners

JULIE NORA

JANA ECHEVARRIA

HEINEMANN
Portsmouth, NH

Heinemann

361 Hanover Street

Portsmouth, NH 03801–3912

www.heinemann.com

Offices and agents throughout the world

The authors and publisher wish to thank those who have generously given permission
to reprint borrowed material:

Excerpts from the Common Core State Standards © Copyright 2010. National
Governors Association Center for Best Practices and Council of Chief State School
Officers. All rights reserved.

Library of Congress Cataloging-in-Publication Data

Names: Nora, Julie. | Echevarría, Jana.
Title: No more low expectations for English learners / Julie Nora and Jana Echevarría.
Description: Portsmouth, NH: Heinemann, 2016. | Series: Not this but that |
   Includes bibliographical references.
Identifiers: LCCN 2016017803 | ISBN 9780325074719
Subjects: LCSH: English language—Study and teaching—Foreign speakers.
Classification: LCC PE1128.A2 N643 2016 | DDC 428.0071—dc23
LC record available at https://lccn.loc.gov/2016017803

Series editors: Ellin Oliver Keene *and* Nell K. Duke
Editor: Margaret LaRaia
Production editor: Sonja S. Chapman
Interior design: Suzanne Heiser
Cover design: Lisa A. Fowler
Typesetter: Valerie Levy, Drawing Board Studios
Manufacturing: Veronica Bennett

Printed in the United States of America on acid-free paper
20   19   18   VP   3   4   5

CONTENTS

Introduction Ellin Oliver Keene   vii

SECTION 1   **NOT THIS**
No More Deficit-Oriented
Instruction
Julie Nora

We Deny English Learners Access When We . . .   2

- *Don't Gear Instruction Toward College Readiness*   2

- *Don't Give Students Access to Mainstream Classes*   2

- *Mistake Language Development with Lack of Effort*   3

- *Don't Give Students Opportunities to Use Language While They Are Learning Language*   3

- *Don't Incorporate Explicit Language Teaching with Content Instruction*   4

- *Limit Our Teaching to Basic Skills*   4

- *Focus Solely on Vocabulary*   4

- *Ignore the Progression of Language Development*   4

- *Ignore the Need to Learn About and Affirm Student Identity*   5

- *Don't Communicate with Their Families*   5

- *Insist on English-Only Policies*   6

- *Overidentify English Learners for Special Education*   6

- *Underidentify English Learners for Special Education*   6

Seeing English Learners Through a Deficit Lens   6

Education Should Promise Opportunity   7

SECTION 2 **WHY NOT? WHAT WORKS?**

9

Why Having High Expectations Matters and How to Support Academic Achievement

Jana Echevarria

Does Teacher Attitude Affect Student Achievement? 10

- *Asset Orientation* 12

How Long Does It Take to Learn Academic English? 18

- *Explicit English Language Teaching* 20

What Supports Are Necessary for Providing Access to Grade-Level Content? 23

- *The SIOP Professional Development Framework* 28

Summary 35

Section 3 **BUT THAT**

37

Teaching from an Asset Perspective

Julie Nora

Students Are More Than "English Learners" 38

- *Affirm Student Identity* 40

Learning Is Language-Based 49

- *Value and Build on Students' Native Languages* 50

- *Model and Create Opportunities to Use Academic Language* 54

- *Provide Feedback That Recognizes Approximation* 58

- *Use Wait Time* 60

- *Create a Safe Classroom Environment That Values Risk-Taking* 62

- *Teach Self-Advocacy* 64

- *Establish and Monitor Language Expectations* 65

High Expectations Through Access to Grade-Level Content 69

- *Build Background Knowledge* 69

- *Teach Thinking Strategies* 73

Afterword Nell K. Duke 77

References 79

INTRODUCTION

ELLIN OLIVER KEENE

"Can English learners (ELs) really learn complex academic content when they are struggling to learn a new language?"

"Should English learners spend their days in the classroom with their age peers, or is it better for them to learn alongside other ELs most of the time?"

"How do I differentiate adequately for ELs in the regular classroom without impeding other students' learning?"

"How long should it take an English learner to become proficient in English?"

In my work with teachers around the country, I believe I have encountered more questions about working with English learners than any other topic. Teachers ask these questions because they want to better serve children who are learning English. And the wide variety of heritage languages in some schools can feel overwhelming, leading many teachers to ask, "How can I possibly teach children who speak so many different languages—Farsi, Mandarin, Portuguese, Hmong—all together with my English-speaking children in a regular academic classroom?"

Reread the questions I pose above. You may sniff a subtle and very troubling strand of doubt that runs through each: are ELs *capable* of learning alongside their English-speaking peers? Perhaps we should pull them out of the regular classroom. Maybe they are holding the rest of our students back. Think of the deleterious impact those doubts will have on students over the course of their K–12 experience. Clearly, we might need to rethink our expectations every bit as much as we might wish to improve our teaching practices.

After reading Julie and Jana's book, I'd like to add my own to the chorus of questions: Why don't we view children who speak more than one language as assets in our classrooms, as gifts to those who speak one language?

I have been honored to work with Julie Nora and Jana Echevarria on this timely and important book. The intersection of Julie's vast experience working with ELs and leading schools that serve them and Jana's twenty years as a researcher and her comprehensive knowledge of the research in this area will soon clear the fog around effective pedagogy for ELs. Together, they tackle the myths that have spread related to teaching ELs and provide numerous examples of teaching practices that capitalize on the richness of culture, language, and perspective our ELs bring to our schools. As Julie reminds us, "Some of the world's most celebrated artists and writers—Vladimir Nabokov, Joseph Conrad, and Salvador Dali, to name only a few—know more than one language and have lived in a variety of cultures."

You're about to learn numerous tactics and approaches to use immediately with ELs (and, by the way, your other students), and you'll have new insights about diverse learners when you close this book. We know that you want your ELs to achieve, and we know you'll have the means to support them in meeting higher expectations. We—my coeditor Nell Duke and Margaret LaRaia, our indefatigable editor at Heinemann, and I—are delighted to bring this book to you and your colleagues, and we know that Julie and Jana have made an important and lasting contribution to the field. We are grateful.

No More Low Expectations for English Learners

SECTION 1

NOT THIS

No More Deficit-Oriented Instruction

JULIE NORA

Too often English learners (ELs)—the students in our schools who are in the process of learning English[1]—are described by what they cannot do: they cannot speak English, they are not prepared for mainstream classrooms, they do not understand the culture of schools in the United States, their parents don't speak English and cannot help them with their schoolwork, they do not do as well academically, and so on. Even the official term *limited English proficient* consigns these students' academic identity to a negative label of diminished capacity. These feelings are only increased by standardized tests and teacher evaluation, and we become trapped in a cycle of limiting potential.

---

1. There are a variety of terms used to describe ELs such as English language learners and dual language learners. Here we use the term *English learners* (ELs).

Of course, there are real challenges in teaching ELs in a language they have not yet mastered. Teachers need to use a variety of strategies to scaffold instruction. Many teachers of ELs have good intentions but lack specific knowledge of the complexities of teaching grade-level contents and language. In this section, I will talk about how easily that knowledge gap can be filled with deficit-based teaching practices. I share stories of well-intentioned teachers whose teaching practices unintentionally communicate low expectations and deny ELs access to the education we want for them and that they deserve.

We Deny English Learners Access When We . . .

. . . Don't Gear Instruction Toward College Readiness

When I enrolled my niece in a suburban high school, I met with Mr. Mark, a guidance counselor. My niece had just come to the United States from a rural part of Venezuela and did not speak any English. Mr. Mark said he would only enroll her in nonacademic classes (physical education, art, music) so that she could learn to speak English. He explained, "I have a long history of working with these students. You've got to get them to talk before they do anything else." He did not explain how my niece would get the coursework necessary to apply to college in four years. In fact, he made it clear that he did not believe applying to college was in my niece's future.

. . . Don't Give Students Access to Mainstream Classes

Ms. Samuels' school recently saw an increase in ELs, which meant that for the first time, she was teaching students who had recently met the criteria to exit their EL program. Because these students still did not have the same level of language skills as their native English-speaking peers, she believed they did not belong in her mainstream classroom. She set up a meeting with her administrator to request that the students be transferred back to an EL class—where they would not have access to content instruction—until they reached the same level of language proficiency as their native English-speaking peers.

. . . Mistake Language Development with Lack of Effort

With no prior experience speaking English, seventh grader Daniela arrived at Cunningham Middle School and impressed her teachers by using English within only a few months. Daniela's teachers were pleased and surprised by her enthusiasm for speaking English, even when she was around speakers of her native language. Within a year, Daniela was comfortable socializing in English. But after three years, her teachers questioned her effort. Daniela still struggled with the academic English required for school. Her teachers were convinced this was happening because Daniela had stopped applying herself.

For more on how academic language develops

see Section 2, page 18

. . . Don't Give Students Opportunities to Use Language While They Are Learning Language

Ms. Vostry knew that language learners go through a "silent period," when they are learning to speak a new language. In an attempt to honor this reticence, she decided that her ELs would only have to listen to English in class and not be required to speak it. She intentionally limited ELs' participation in academic talk: calling almost exclusively on native English speakers in whole-class settings and assigning ELs to the nonspeaking role (like note taker) in partner and small-group work. She expressed surprise that ELs did not grow beyond the silent phase in her class.

. . . Don't Incorporate Explicit Language Teaching with Content Instruction

Science teacher Ms. Angelo was concerned that Marquis, an EL, did not talk in class and had difficulty writing. When one of her colleagues asked

> **To find positive specific examples of each of these**
>
> see Section 3

how much scaffolding and explicit language instruction she had provided, Ms. Angelo responded, "I am a science teacher, not a language teacher. I have a lot of science content to cover and do not have the time to teach language."

. . . Limit Our Teaching to Basic Skills

Ms. Jen had her seventh-grade ELs practice cursive by tracing letters and then words on worksheets. The handouts also included sentences, but none of the students completed this part of the worksheet. The teacher, when asked why, responded: "These students need to learn to write cursive before they can write a sentence."

. . . Focus Solely on Vocabulary

Mr. Klein was so committed to expanding the vocabulary of his ELs that it became his near-exclusive focus. Every object in the classroom was labeled. Each week, students were assigned a new list of fifty words to look up and define, on which they were tested at the end of the week.

. . . Ignore the Progression of Language Development

Ms. Carey was concerned with the spelling errors of second grader Lucila. On two pages of math word problems, Ms. Carey circled each of Lucila's spelling errors and made her rewrite all of her responses. The word problems were solved correctly and the misspelled words were comprehensible (and developmentally appropriate for her age and stage of language development). Lucila's teacher wanted the best for her—to spell correctly—but was misguided in focusing Lucila's attention away from the math content. In fear of spelling errors, Lucila wrote shorter responses and thought less deeply about the math concepts. She began to dislike math.

. . . Ignore the Need to Learn About and Affirm Student Identity

At Marshall High School, the teachers and administrators do not share the cultural and linguistic backgrounds of most of their students, many of whom are recent immigrants. In the annual school survey (required by the state's Department of Education), students and their families said they did not feel welcome or understood by the teachers and administrators. Faculty were surprised and frustrated by this feedback and responded with comments like, "How are we expected to understand the cultures of all of our students, they come from so many different places?" and "Our job is to teach them, not to get to know them."

> There are a variety of ways of getting to know our ELs that start with but include more than our individual relationship with a student. We also need to consider how our curriculum and school community recognizes the identities of our students.

. . . Don't Communicate with Their Families

Mr. Michaels regularly communicates with the parents of his students. He wanted to reach out to Elizabeth's parents because he was concerned with her academic performance. He did not because he assumed that they had limited abilities to communicate in English because they had recently moved to the United States and their daughter had not yet fully mastered English. He did not speak their language and did not want to make the parents feel uncomfortable, so he decided to forgo communication and hope for the best for Elizabeth's academic improvement.

. . . *Insist on English-Only Policies*

A middle school teaching team decided to improve the English proficiency of their ELs by committing to an English-only policy in their classrooms. One teacher planned to post a sign with a construction symbol that says, "This is an English-only zone." Another would keep a penalty jar and collect money when a language other than English was spoken or written. Another teacher assigned students the rotating role of "language police."

. . . *Overidentify English Learners for Special Education*

Ms. Sanchez could not tell whether EL student Katy's academic struggle was due to a disability or language. She thought it best to err on the side of caution and decided to refer Katy for a special education evaluation. Katy was given an individualized education program (IEP). Katy's subsequent teachers struggled with knowing whether Katy's difficulty was language or disability and Katy received excessive scaffolding minimizing learning. Four years later, when Katy became proficient in English, her IEP was terminated.

. . . *Underidentify English Learners for Special Education*

José, a seventh grader who had been in the English as a second language (ESL) program since kindergarten, approached me, his ESL teacher, to wonder whether he had a disability and asked how he might get special education services if he needed them. José was completely orally proficient using social language in English, but experienced significant difficulties grasping academic concepts.

Seeing English Learners Through a Deficit Lens

In each of these situations, the educators were trying to address perceived needs of their students. Unfortunately, these educators denied their students access to learning. Many had not received sufficient professional preparation in how to teach students who are in the process of learning English or who have not yet mastered it. Their schools may not have been equipped with faculty members who spoke the languages of their students and may not have had interpreters or materials to facilitate communication. They were communicating low expectations, limiting access to higher-order thinking or academic content, and, in other cases, access to language learning.

Education Should Promise Opportunity

My niece's guidance counselor believed she was not capable of learning academic content because she did not speak English. He demonstrated a common and mistaken belief that EL students will learn English by being in classes with low-level academic expectations (art, music, physical education). In fact, students need structured opportunities to develop their language skills. Exposure is important, but so is explicit instruction. Oral skills do not absolutely precede literacy skills; they develop synergistically. When he denied her access to academic classes, he was denying the opportunity to develop the language and cognitive skills she needed. If I had agreed to his plan, she would not have received the course work she needed to apply to college. Before meeting her and without giving her the opportunity afforded by instruction, he had decided she was not college material. (Know that I interceded and my niece is now a bilingual teacher.) Too many EL students and their families learn—too late—in eleventh or twelfth grade that they had not been given access to the course work they needed to apply to college. Even more tragic is that many parents immigrate to the United States to ensure their child has the opportunity to attend college.

When Ms. Samuels wanted ELs removed from her class until they were proficient in English, she was confusing language proficiency with capacity to learn grade-level content. Regardless of language proficiency, ELs need access to grade-level content. In Sections 2 and 3, you'll see how teachers can do this in manageable, achievable ways. It takes longer to develop academic language proficiency than to acquire social language. Access without support is not sufficient. ELs need daily, active opportunities to practice academic language skills in the context of learning content.

When Katy's teacher identified her struggle with language as a learning disability and when Jose's teachers overlooked his disability because he was acquiring language, the teachers did not understand developmental phases of acquiring a new language.

All learners, English speakers and ELs, benefit from explicit language instruction to engage in the higher-order thinking required to learn new content, but science teacher Ms. Angelo didn't yet understand this. When teachers like Mr. Klein focus on cursive or vocabulary in isolation, they decontextualize language learning, which increases the likelihood that ELs will disengage.

We may recognize ourselves in these examples. That may feel uncomfortable and make us want to disengage. That's how the teachers at Marshall High School felt when they learned how EL families felt about their school. That's how Mr. Michaels felt when he imagined having to deal with the discomfort of Elizabeth's parents. These kinds of conversations require a willingness to be vulnerable—to question whether our instruction is increasing our ELs' access to academic opportunity or diminishing it and to ask for help when we're not certain or overwhelmed. This book provides a framework of understandings and practices to make you a more capable teacher of ELs. Let's now move to Section 2 and explore the research on teaching ELs.

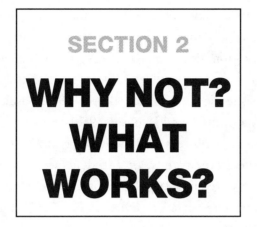

WHY NOT? WHAT WORKS?

Why Having High Expectations Matters and How to Support Academic Achievement

JANA ECHEVARRIA

At Christa McAuliffe Elementary School, a large urban school with high numbers of English learners, students are greeted at the front gate each morning by the principal, Keisha Washington, who calls many children and their parent by name. "Have a productive day!" is Ms. Washington's typical phrase of encouragement. Children pass by posters in the hallways with inspirational sayings, such as "Do what you can, with what you have, where you are—Theodore Roosevelt" and "An hour of hard practice is worth five hours of foot-dragging—Pancho Segura." In each classroom is a sign that says "We are achievers!" which reflects both the school's motto and the teachers' attitudes toward students. Efforts such as these may seem trivial but studies show that the expectations educators hold for students indeed make a difference.

Does Teacher Attitude Affect Student Achievement?

Decades of research demonstrates that teachers' expectations, attitudes, and behaviors toward certain students—typically students of color and those from disadvantaged backgrounds—have a direct and profound impact on the way these students see themselves as learners and on their academic performance (Brophy 1983; Boser, Wilhelm, and Hanna 2014; ; Rosenthal and Jacobson 1968).

Rosenthal and Jacobson's study (1968) was the first to draw attention to the issue. In their study, after students were tested to measure their IQs, some were randomly chosen and labeled "growth spurters" and their names were given to the teachers. At the end of the academic year, students were retested and those labeled as growth spurters showed a more significant increase in test scores than the students not thought to be growth spurters. After years of debate and further study, the conclusion is that although teacher expectation probably doesn't affect IQ, it does affect students' achievement (Spitz 1999). Students are more engaged in the learning process when teachers have high expectations for them, and they learn more (Cooper and Tom 1984).

> **Research like this demands that we take a hard look at our attitude toward the English learners in our classroom and school and consider how we might shift to a more positive, asset-based perspective.**

In Brophy's seminal work on teacher expectations (1983), he found that teachers behaved differently toward students for whom they had high expectations than they did toward students for whom they had low expectations. For example, teachers:

- typically offered high-expectancy students feedback on assignments at a higher rate than they offered it to low-expectancy students (97 percent and 85 percent, respectively)
- sought improved responses from high-expectancy students when they answered incorrectly and simply moved on when low-expectancy students answered incorrectly

- waited less time for low-expectancy students to answer questions
- smiled less and offered less eye contact to low-expectancy students.

Subsequent research confirmed Brophy's findings and revealed additional ways teachers behave when they have low expectations for students (Haycock 2001; Marzano 2010). Some of these behaviors include:

- calling upon them less often
- asking them less challenging questions
- delving into their answers less deeply
- rewarding them for less rigorous responses
- giving them fewer and less challenging assignments.

The early studies as well as more recent research found that most often the students for whom teachers had low expectations were students of color and those from disadvantaged backgrounds. Approximately two-thirds of English learners, considered students of color, are from low-income backgrounds and have parents with limited formal education (Garcia, Jensen, and Scribner 2009). These students are at significant risk for being subjected to the teacher behaviors listed earlier and for not being provided the kind of challenging academic opportunities that lead to high achievement.

One reason teachers may not ask English learners challenging questions or delve further into their responses is that they believe that low English proficiency prohibits them from participating fully in lessons. Actually, English learners are as capable as other students to think at high cognitive levels about complex ideas and topics. Just because they may struggle to express their ideas in English doesn't mean they aren't engaged intellectually in the lesson, especially when instruction is scaffolded to ensure comprehension. For example, a student may have a strong background in math but doesn't understand the English instructions or word problems, or the actual computation process may differ from the way the student was taught previously. Or, an English

The research cited here is just one example of how having English learners in your classroom can be an asset for all your students.

learner understands the lesson's concepts due to the support provided (e.g., use of multimedia) but is unable to express her understanding adequately in English. Not only are English learners as capable of learning as their English-speaking counterparts, research shows that dual language learners actually have *higher* meta-linguistic awareness than monolingual learners (Bialystok 1988, 1999, 2001), giving these students an advantage.

Although teachers may have difficulty changing their expectations because their beliefs, attitudes, and biases toward certain types of students have developed over the years, what actually communicates expectations to students are teacher *behaviors*, such as those specified earlier. The good news is that teacher behavior can change (Marzano 2010).

Asset Orientation

The issue of effective instructional programs for English learners is a present and urgent concern in the United States because of their large and growing numbers. During the 2010–11 school year, there were over five million English learners in schools, and the number nationwide has increased more than 10 percent in the past decade. English learners bring a number of assets and resources to the classroom that often go unrecognized by teachers and other school staff. These students come to school already speaking a variety of home languages, most commonly Spanish, Vietnamese, Chinese, Arabic, or Hmong, and should be provided the opportunity to use the languages in their linguistic repertoires to think about the world, to research topics, to take notes, to write an essay, and for other academic purposes (Bauer 2009; Moll, Saez, and Dworin 2001). When students are able to use both their home language and English in school, not only will they achieve at similar levels as monolingual students (August et al. 2006) but they will also recognize their home language as the resource it is. As former Secretary of Education Arne Duncan (2014) commented, "These languages are significant not only to our economic competitiveness but also to our nation's security. The heritage languages our English learners bring to school are major assets to preserve and value."

In a study of schools with English learner populations, teachers recognized the assets these students bring. The following quotes characterize their attitudes (National Center for Educational Evaluation and Regional Assistance 2014). "The strength they bring is a new perspective; they bring their own experiences from wherever they came from, and it really opens up the room for great conversation to establish everyone's background knowledge . . . they bring their own opinions to the classroom" and "They are very eager learners and very supportive of education and teachers, and they have a high level of motivation from students and families to learn and get the best education they can."

Unfortunately, being valued for their cultural and linguistic diversity is not always the reality for English learners and their families. When asked if they feel welcomed at their child's school when they come to visit, 26 percent of Hispanic parents said they do not, compared to 8 percent of white parents (Perkins-Gough 2008). In contrast, in classrooms and schools where there is a climate that values students and their families, respects their culture and language, and expects all students to achieve high standards, students outperform similar schools that do not have these same conditions and expectations (Bottoms 2007; Echevarria, Short, and Vogt 2008; Nora 2013; Schmoker 2007). Furthermore, the misperception of immigrant students as *pobrecitos* (poor little things) may lead to coddling of nontraditional students, robbing them of challenging learning experiences, rigorous curricula, and academic success (Adger and Locke 2000). There is a related tendency to consider English learners as "almost the same" as English monolinguals except that they are lacking English proficiency. Ruiz (2013) suggests an alternative to thinking of English learners as different from the norm: they are representative of diversity *as the norm* in schools. Demographic trends confirm that diversity in schools *is* the norm but the issue is teachers' attitudes toward the resources these students have to contribute. Teachers should look for opportunities to build on the linguistic and cultural repertoire English learners bring to school and schools should offer a climate that promotes learning and a sense of belonging for students, parents, and school staff.

Based on a review of research on the social, cultural, and family influences on learning, Goldenberg and Coleman (2010) make the following recommendations, which are useful for helping teachers view student differences as assets, tapping into what students bring to the classroom, and valuing their languages and cultures:

- *Bearing in mind the relationship between the reader, the text, and knowledge needed to make the text understandable, use materials whose content has some level of familiarity to English learners (from home culture, pop culture, media, and other experiences).* The important role that background knowledge plays in text comprehension is virtually undisputed (Neuman, Kaefer, and Pinkham 2014). The more background knowledge a reader has that connects with the text being read, the likelier the reader will be able to make sense of what is being read. Goldenberg and Coleman (2010) point to studies that show the same is true for English learners. Culturally familiar materials are those that depict characters and situations that would be known to students from their home experiences, such as traditional cultural tales or traditional family events. However, children also develop background knowledge from everyday learning experiences, not necessarily only those that are culturally influenced. In one study, when elementary English learners knew as much about the topic in the reading passages as English-only students (piñatas and polar bears), both groups performed nearly the same on a test of reading comprehension (Garcia 1991), demonstrating that familiarity with the topic is important in reading comprehension for all students. Teachers also need to bear in mind that English learners may have valuable nontraditional background experiences and understandings that can be brought to bear during literacy instruction. Furthermore, these students develop language and literacy skills in a variety of ways, such as through popular culture materials, and not necessarily only through text-based materials. Unless teachers broaden their view of literacy, some students' unique abilities and understandings of story may not be recognized as legitimate background knowledge (Urbach and Klinger 2012).

- *Observe how students behave with their parents and peers and try to use a similar style to promote student motivation and engagement and avoid misinterpretations of students' behavior.* A study conducted by Au and Mason (1981) demonstrated that when native Hawaiian children were allowed to speak in a way that they were used to at home, which was to speak freely and spontaneously without waiting for the teacher to call on them, their participation in reading changed in a number of ways: their engagement increased, they made more on-topic and correct responses, and the number of ideas they expressed increased. Understanding family interaction patterns and replicating them in the classroom was beneficial to students. On the other hand, it is not unusual for English learners to display behaviors that are considered problematic by teachers but that would be considered a normal response to their individual situations. English learners may be seen as abnormally shy or quiet, or they may act out. Some immigrant students have experienced significant trauma due to strife in their home country or because they are separated from parents and other family members. Other English learners may be responding to the situation of not being able to communicate their wants and needs or from feelings of isolation and rejection by peers and school staff. Teachers need to be cognizant of the impact of language differences on classroom behavior and not draw conclusions prematurely that English learners' behaviors indicate a learning or behavior problem (Santos and Ostrosky 2016).

- *Find ways to involve parents in supporting their children's education.* Parental involvement is a valuable asset, and there are innumerable ways parents can be supportive. The key is communicating with them and working with them to find ways that they can support their children's academic achievement. The benefit of parents' involvement in their children's academic achievement is well documented, and it has also been found that although parents of English learners are willing and mostly able to help with their children's academic achievement, schools "underestimate parents' interest, motivation, and potential contributions" (August and Shanahan 2006, 314). There are a variety of ways for parents to participate in enhancing outcomes for their children, including encouraging parent volunteers in the classroom, maintaining regular communication about school activities and homework assignments, helping at home, and so on. In a study of schools with effective programs for English learners, one elementary school held regularly scheduled after-school "make-and-take" meetings where parents learned, for example, about the importance of reading with their child and made literacy logs for use at home (Echevarria, Short, and Vogt 2008). In Section 3, Julie describes a meaningful follow-up activity to a lesson (see Figure 3–3), which involves students' families. Beyond the obvious benefit of learning about their own families, why they came to Rhode Island, and so forth, students have an opportunity to interact with family members around an academic assignment. That home-school connection is important for both students and their families. Studies have shown that parents of English learners are not sufficiently informed about what they can do to help their child succeed. "By bridging this communication gap, educators are likely to find willing (and grateful) allies" (Goldenberg and Coleman 2010, 132).

- *Consider making home visits to get to know families and their community.* The effort expended will reap rewards in terms of showing you are interested in their children and want to develop a relationship with the family to promote their children's school success. There is a pervasive view of working-class and poor families as contributing to their children's academic and linguistic deficits due to deficiencies in parenting (Dudley-Marling and Michaels 2012). Not only is this view not grounded in scientific evidence, it doesn't offer schools any resolution. In my own experience, home visits provided a wealth of information about my students' and their families' values and cultures, but the experience also opened my eyes to the many assets these parents offered in terms of home-school partnerships. Culturally and linguistically diverse parents care very much about their children's success in school and want them to obtain as much education as possible, even through college (Goldenberg 2006). Many have made significant sacrifices to offer their children a better future (Suarez-Orozco, Suarez-Orozco, and Todorova 2008). Remember: "No child profits from a perspective that portrays her, her family, or her community as deprived or deficient" (Dudley-Marling and Michaels 2012, 6).

Too often teachers fail to recognize not only the assets that students bring but also the important role they themselves play in building on those assets so that English learners can achieve academically and develop their academic English skills. It is not unusual for teachers to be focused solely on students becoming English proficient and to become concerned by the amount of time it takes English learners to advance in language proficiency, usually because they don't understand the complexity of developing a second language.

How Long Does It Take to Learn Academic English?

It is often said that if you want to learn a language, you should go to the country to be immersed in it. Then why aren't English learners quickly learning English? Actually, students typically do "pick up" social language relatively quickly through exposure to the language. They learn how to interact with English-speaking peers and teachers; they can recount what they did over the weekend, ask socially appropriate questions, and tell the teacher why their homework is late. Even so, exposure and interaction alone aren't sufficient for native-like accuracy (Lyster 2007). Some aspects of social language require explicit instruction such as how to ask for clarification, apologize, politely disagree, and make requests (Short and Echevarria 2016). But even as English learners acquire conversational or social language, it isn't sufficient for school tasks because it differs from academic language (Cummins 1981).

Academic English proficiency takes longer to attain and is a more complex process than acquiring social language. Academic language and literacy skills are fundamental for school success because age-appropriate knowledge of English is necessary for understanding content standards and accessing grade-level core content. Academic language is used across content areas for tasks such as synthesizing information, predicting outcomes, comparing ideas, and describing processes. In short, it is the language of school. Some examples of academic language skills required by the Common Core State Standards include:

- Prepare for and participate in an academic discussion.
- Use questions to connect ideas from several speakers.
- Move from explaining one's own ideas to explaining the ideas of others.
- Summarize and synthesize points of disagreement.
- Delineate and evaluate the argument and specific claims in a text.
- Make logical inferences from the meaning of the text.

- Cite specific textual evidence when writing or speaking to support conclusions drawn from the text.
- Determine central ideas or themes of a text and analyze their development.
- Summarize the key supporting details and ideas.

These skills are challenging for many students but even more so for English learners who are still mastering the English language, including its grammar and vocabulary. Think about it from your own experience. If you have conversational ability in another language, imagine being expected to evaluate an argument and specific claims in an academic text. First, being able to comprehend the text well enough to understand the argument put forth would be quite challenging. Then, to be able to think about the argument (or claims) in the text, understand it, and evaluate its veracity would take a level of sophistication that students at the beginning or even intermediate levels of English proficiency couldn't achieve without significant supports.

For specific examples of how to structure meaningful opportunities for academic talk

see Section 3, page 68

Saunders and Goldenberg (2010) summarized key findings from a synthesis of research on educating English learners (Genesee et al. 2006) as follows:

- It takes English learners four to six years to achieve "early advanced" proficiency (level 4, where level 1 is beginning and level 5 is advanced proficiency).
- Average oral English proficiency reached level 5 (nativelike proficiency) by grade 5 in fewer than half of the studies analyzed.
- Beginning speakers advance to middle levels of proficiency fairly quickly, but progress from middle to upper levels of proficiency (levels 3 to 5) is considerably slower. That is, many English learners get "stuck" once they reach a middle level of English proficiency and make little progress thereafter.

One "takeaway" message from the research is that it takes time—considerable time—to attain English proficiency. Even though students may converse quite well in English on the playground, in hallways, and during small talk before class, it does not mean that they have mastered the academic language of school. Some teachers mistakenly believe that students are not putting forth the effort necessary for completing academic tasks because they "speak English," but that is confusing issues of motivation with language acquisition (Echevarria and Short 2010). The reality is that students require scaffolds or supports for many years, especially because as students progress through the grade levels, language demands increase significantly. It is typical to see fairly steady progress initially because language demands are less. In the early grades, substantial context is provided by teachers and texts in the form of visuals, gestures, demonstrations, manipulatives, and other forms of support that make the message comprehensible. As students move up the grades, however, there tends to be less support provided at the same time that the complexity of language increases. English learners are not likely to acquire the English language they need to be successful in school without an explicit focus on teaching them about how English works and how to use it to achieve high academic standards.

Explicit English Language Teaching

Explicit English language development (ELD) or English as a second language (ESL) teaching needs to be a part of daily instruction for English learners to advance in their English proficiency. If English learners don't learn, for example, forms and structures of academic language, they will continue to plateau at the intermediate level of English proficiency for years, becoming what is called "long-term English learners" (Olsen 2010). Long-term English learners, or LTELs, are those students who remain English learners for more than five or six years. There are tens of thousands of LTELs in schools across the United States, with nearly 60 percent of secondary English learners in this category (Olsen 2010). These students need teaching that focuses on specific aspects of

English coupled with opportunities to use academic English in meaningful ways.

During ELD instruction, English is the focus, with content material used as the vehicle for learning about English. (In some ESL or ELD classes, the time is used as a tutoring session to keep up with students' content area assignments. However, in the long run, this does a disservice to English learners because although they may complete a given assignment, they aren't learning the foundational skills needed to be fluent English speakers.) Students have opportunities to practice the four domains—reading, writing, speaking, and listening—using grade-level materials. For example, when students are studying the muscular system in science, during ELD time they might practice key terms using complete sentences, as seen in the activity in Figure 2–1, Find Someone Who. This kind of activity reinforces learning that

Figure 2–1   Find Someone Who

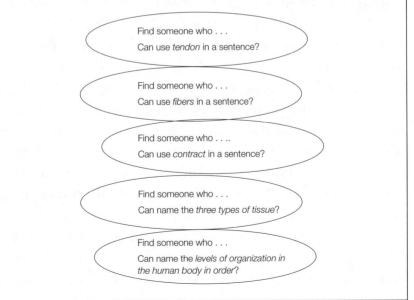

Directions: Mix throughout the classroom and find a partner with whom you do not usually work. Person A asks a question from the worksheet and Person B responds. Person A writes down B's answer on his or her or own worksheet. Person B checks and initials the answer. Then, Person B asks a question from the worksheet and Person A responds. Person B records the answer on his or her worksheet. Person A checks and initials the answer. Partners shake hands and search for a new partner. Repeat steps until worksheets are complete.

Find someone who . . .
Can use *tendon* in a sentence?

Find someone who . . .
Can use *fibers* in a sentence?

Find someone who . . ..
Can use *contract* in a sentence?

Find someone who . . .
Can name the *three types of tissue*?

Find someone who . . .
Can name the *levels of organization in the human body in order*?

has taken place in the content class or during a previous ELD lesson. In this example, students are already familiar with the terms and concepts related to the muscular system and have the definitions written in their science vocabulary notebooks. The Find Someone Who activity serves a number of purposes. First, it gets students up, moving around, and actively engaged with the material, which is more effective than simply being asked to memorize information (Jensen 2008). Second, students are practicing academic English in authentic ways by interacting with peers and asking and answering questions. Finally, English learners are gaining practice in reading, writing, speaking, and listening using terms that they need to know and use in content classes.

Other activities during ELD time might include focused, explicit instruction in the standards-based skills listed previously, such as how to summarize text or evaluate an argument. Students should be provided with plenty of practice using the target skill.

However, focused ELD alone isn't enough. Students need opportunities to learn and practice English skills throughout the day in content lessons in addition to the set time for ELD. We cannot expect students to attain advanced or nativelike proficiency with only a given number of minutes per day spent on explicit academic language development.

In reality, with rigorous content standards, all students are learning academic English, native English speakers and English learners alike. When teachers address a lesson's language demands, it is beneficial for all students—but critical for English learners. Rigorous grade-level lessons expose students to academic language, and the use of appropriate supports makes that language accessible. For example, when teaching students to navigate informational text, all students need practice citing text evidence, using describing words, and using text-specific vocabulary. Effective teachers explicitly teach these skills and, for English learners, provide supports for using academic language such as a word bank and sentence frames. Word banks, or word walls, contain key terms that students need to know and use during a lesson or unit of study. They may take on a variety of forms, including writing words and/or phrases for students to see on a whiteboard or butcher paper, PowerPoint slides, or laminated posters hanging in the classroom, or they may be in the form of individual word notebooks. Whatever form they take, word banks can be an important resource for English learners. Students should be encouraged to use word banks as a reference to support their learning. Sentence frames are used as supports for expressing ideas orally and in writing. They scaffold students' thinking and use of academic language by providing a frame, or partially completed sentence. For example, an elementary math frame might be, "An estimate is a guess. My estimate is _____." Or, for oral discussions, "I disagree with _____ because _____."

Providing supports for English learners need not be daunting for teachers, but it does require thoughtful planning so that lessons contain features that enable all students to use academic language appropriately to make academic progress.

What Supports Are Necessary for Providing Access to Grade-Level Content?

English learners need to have instruction adjusted for them so that they have equal access to grade-level learning. By definition, English learners are in the process of acquiring English, the language of instruction, so the curriculum and instruction must be modified to meet their needs (August and Shanahan 2010). Teaching that provides the supports English learners need to understand the content and to improve their language proficiency is commonly referred to as *sheltered instruction* (Freeman and Freeman 1988). The purpose of sheltered instruction is to deliver grade-level subject matter content (language arts, math, science, social studies, health, and art) in a manner that is accessible to all learners. In sheltered instruction classes, instruction is delivered by a core teacher and is drawn from grade-level curricula. The teacher scaffolds or supports the content learning by using a variety of techniques and strategies for making information comprehensible to students. At the same time, sheltered lessons help develop student language skills across the four domains: reading, writing, speaking and listening (Cloud, Genesee, and Hamayan 2009; Goldenberg and Coleman 2010).

A widely used research-validated model of sheltered instruction is the Sheltered Instruction Observation Protocol (SIOP) Model, a framework for lesson planning and delivery (Echevarria, Vogt, and Short 2017). As you can see in Figure 2–2, the SIOP Model has many features recommended for high-quality instruction for all students, such as collaborative group work, reading comprehension strategies, and differentiated instruction. However, the model adds key features for the academic success of English learners, such as including language objectives in every content lesson, providing ample opportunities for oral language practice, developing content-related vocabulary and background knowledge, and emphasizing academic literacy. It is not a step-by-step approach but rather a framework for organizing research-based practices.

Adjusting instruction to make it more comprehensible for English learners and to increase their participation in lessons is critical. Sometimes teachers underestimate English learners' ability to take part in rigorous, standards-based lessons and to engage in higher-order thinking. In fact, studies have found that English learners are capable of full participation in grade-level lessons. One study where teachers who received SIOP professional development, held grade-level expectations for middle school English learners, and scaffolded their learning found improvement in the quality of writing produced by students compared with those whose teachers didn't receive SIOP professional development (students were mostly low socioeconomic status with a variety of home languages; over 50 percent were Spanish-speaking) (Echevarria, Short, and Powers 2006). In the study, teachers implementing SIOP lessons maintained a high level of discourse and asked higher-

To find a variety of instructional examples from different content areas

see Section 3

Figure 2–2   Features of the SIOP Model

The SIOP Model
(Sheltered Instruction Observation Protocol)

Lesson Preparation

1. *Content objectives* clearly defined, displayed, and reviewed with students

2. *Language objectives* clearly defined, displayed, and reviewed with students

3. *Content concepts* appropriate for age and educational background level of students

4. *Supplementary materials* used to a high degree, making the lesson clear and meaningful (e.g., computer programs, graphs, models, visuals)

5. *Adaptation of content* (e.g., text, assignment) to all levels of student proficiency

6. *Meaningful activities* that integrate lesson concepts (e.g., surveys, letter writing, simulations, constructing models) with language practice opportunities for reading, writing, listening, and/or speaking

Building Background

7. *Concepts explicitly linked* to students' background experiences

8. *Links explicitly made* between past learning and new concepts

9. *Key vocabulary emphasized* (e.g., introduced, written, repeated, and highlighted for students to see)

Comprehensible Input

10. *Speech* appropriate for students' proficiency levels (e.g., slower rate, enunciation, and simple sentence structure for beginners)

11. *Clear explanation* of academic tasks

12. *A variety of techniques* used to make content concepts clear (e.g., modeling, visuals, hands-on activities, demonstrations, gestures, body language)

(continues)

Figure 2–2 *(continued)*

The SIOP Model
(Sheltered Instruction Observation Protocol)

Strategies

13. Ample opportunities provided for students to use *learning strategies*

14. *Scaffolding techniques* consistently used, assisting and supporting student understanding (e.g., think-alouds)

15. A variety of *questions or tasks that promote higher-order thinking skills* (e.g., literal, analytical, and interpretive questions)

Interaction

16. Frequent opportunities for *interaction* and discussion between teacher and student and among students, which encourage elaborated responses about lesson concepts

17. *Grouping configurations* that support language and content objectives of the lesson

18. Sufficient *wait time for student responses* consistently provided

19. Ample opportunities for students to *clarify key concepts in L1* as needed with aide, peer, or L1 text

Practice & Application

20. *Hands-on materials and/or manipulatives* provided for students to practice using new content knowledge

21. Activities provided for students to *apply content and language knowledge* in the classroom

22. Activities integrate all *language skills* (i.e., reading, writing, listening, and speaking)

Lesson Delivery

23. *Content objectives* clearly supported by lesson delivery

24. *Language objectives* clearly supported by lesson delivery

25. *Students engaged* approximately 90% to 100% of the period

26. *Pacing* of the lesson appropriate to students' ability levels

Review & Assessment

27. Comprehensive *review of key vocabulary*

28. Comprehensive *review of key content concepts*

29. Regular *feedback* provided to students on their output (e.g., language, content, work)

30. *Assessment of student comprehension and learning* of all lesson objectives (e.g., spot checking, group response) throughout the lesson

Echevarria, Jana L.; Vogt, MaryEllen; Short, Deborah J., *Making Content Comprehensible for English Learners: The SIOP Model, 5th Ed.*, © 2017, pp. 309–311. Reprinted by permission of Pearson Education, Inc., New York.

order questions but student responses were scaffolded through the use of sentence frames. In a sheltered history class, for example, the teacher asked groups to work together and decide what the greatest achievement of the Persian Empire was. Each group read several different passages about four achievements or inventions, discussed and classified each achievement, wrote information about each one, and decided on the one they thought was the greatest or most important. Then each group reported its conclusion. The teacher provided sentence frames to facilitate the oral report (see Figure 2–3).

Figure 2–3   Sentence Frame

The greatest achievement of the Persian Empire was _____

because _____. It was more important than others

because _____.

In this way, English learners were required to read and write about grade-level ideas, analyze and compare achievements, and evaluate which was most important—all higher-order thinking skills using academic discourse. The structure of the lesson made the language and thinking required manageable, especially the provision of sentence frames as a scaffold for those who needed it.

When teachers consistently implement the instructional features we know are effective for English learners, student performance improves, as does language proficiency. A study replicated and scaled up the afore-mentioned Echevarria, Short, and Powers (2006) research with English learners in grades 6–12. Results indicated that students with SIOP-trained teachers made statistically significant gains in their average mean scores on the state's English language proficiency assessment for oral language, writing, and total proficiency, compared to the comparison group (Short, Fidelman, and Louguit 2012).

Furthermore, in a program of studies at the National Center for Research on the Educational Achievement and Teaching of English Learners (CREATE), researchers conducted separate studies in a variety of middle school content areas. In one of the studies in science classes, it was found that the more consistently teachers used features of the SIOP Model, elaborated below, the better students performed (Echevarria, et al. 2011). So, it is not enough for teachers to pick and choose among effective instructional techniques; students benefit from consistent, systematic implementation in every lesson. In the final two years of CREATE, the separate studies were integrated into a schoolwide intervention with an overarching framework of SIOP professional development and weekly coaching sessions (Center for Research on the Educational Achievement and Teaching of English Language Learners 2012). Students in the intervention classes, those that were language-rich and provided access to the core curriculum, outperformed students who were in control classes on standardized tests. They also outperformed in criterion-based measures of content knowledge and academic English for both English learners and native English speakers in the treatment classes (Short and Himmel 2013).

The SIOP Professional Development Framework

Teachers in the studies discussed previously received professional development in designing and implementing SIOP lessons. The content of the professional development focused on the following components of instruction for English learners.

Lesson Preparation

Include posting content and language objectives for every lesson so both teachers and students are cognizant of the lesson's purpose and its language focus.

Content objectives identify what students will learn and be able to do in a lesson, and language objectives address the aspects of academic language that will be developed or reinforced. In writing language objectives, teachers consider the key vocabulary, concept words, or other terms students need to talk, read, and write about the lesson's topic. Also, consider the grammatical forms or language structures that are common to the content area and provide practice opportunities. Finally, think about the language skills necessary for students to accomplish the lesson's tasks, such as reading to identify specific information or reporting an observation.

Building Background

Include key vocabulary: tapping into students' background knowledge and experience to make lessons relevant and meaningful; developing background including vocabulary.

Many English learners have gaps in their academic knowledge and skills for a number of reasons, such as interrupted schooling, mobility, or ineffective teaching. Teachers need to plan activities that provide the necessary background information to make the lesson meaningful. For example, students might be asked to act out a vocabulary term that represents a concept in the lesson (e.g., distressed or ecstatic) or experience it (e.g., having students *contract* their muscles). Because of the important relationship between vocabulary knowledge and reading comprehension (Hiebert and Kamil 2005), it is critical that teachers include activities and opportunities for English learners to deepen their knowledge of academic English words and to use them in content areas. In a typical lesson, the specific content vocabulary terms are written for students to see and use for reference. Because these words are so specific to the lesson's academic context and not normally encountered in everyday English, they need to be explicitly taught. Effective lessons also include activities where students interact with the words in multiple ways. Figure 2–4 shows a more elaborate word bank page, one that provides context for each word. In this example, the teacher models the process of completing the vocabulary page followed by having students practice the process. They first write the word and its definition, then select a word-learning strategy of their choice: imagery, spider map, synonym and antonym, or context. The strategy is then represented in the box. The completed page is added to their word bank notebook.

Figure 2–4 **Vocabulary Worksheet**

Word	**Definition**
Strategy Checklist: Check the box of the strategy you will use to remember the word. ❏ Imagery (draw a picture) ❏ Spider Map (body is the word, details and examples are the legs) ❏ Synonym and antonym (same/opposite) ❏ Context (use the word in an original sentence)	
In the box, show how you are using this strategy.	

Comprehensible Input

Use a variety of techniques to make the content concepts clear and understandable such as multimedia, demonstrations, gestures, and hands-on activities.

If information is presented in a way that students cannot understand, such as an explanation that is spoken too rapidly, or reading selections that are far above students' reading levels with no visuals or graphic organizers to assist them, many English learners will be unable to learn the content necessary to attain high academic standards. In an effective lesson, teachers actively engage students by making the lesson's meaning understandable. However, reducing the complexity of language is only effective when used judiciously. Oversimplification of spoken and written language limits exposure to appropriately challenging material such as varied sentence constructions and language forms (Crossley et al. 2007). As we've discussed earlier in this section, it takes time to become proficient in a new language, and to advance in English proficiency, English learners require significant "clues" to augment oral and written input. Technology affords a wealth of resources to assist in making lessons comprehensible, but simple techniques such as repetition, speaking with clear enunciation, and gesturing are also effective.

Strategies

Promote higher-order thinking through questioning and tasks that require more than low-level thinking.

This component addresses student learning strategies, teacher-scaffolded instruction, and higher-order thinking skills. Some English learners aren't familiar with learning strategies such as predicting and inferring, generating questions to guide comprehension, and visualizing. Thus they require explicit instruction in how to use learning strategies flexibly and in combination (Ardasheva and Tretter 2012; Dole et al. 1991). In fact, teaching learning strategies has a long history of research supporting its efficacy (Vaughn, Gersten, and Chard 2000). Effective teaching also includes asking English learners a range of questions, many of which require higher levels of thinking (Genesee et al. 2006). It is easy to ask simple, factual questions; however, teachers must go beyond questions that can be answered with a one- or two-word response and instead ask questions and create projects or tasks that require students to think more critically and apply their language skills in a more extended way. Their answers may contain few words but those words represent complex thinking. For example, the activity in Section 3 (shown in Figure 3–4) provides the opportunity for students to use higher-level skills by making predictions about settling in a remote location. Students compare and contrast information read from the text, clarify their understanding, and apply new knowledge.

Interaction

Provide frequent opportunities for students to interact with one another in collaborative discussions.

In an effective lesson, students have ample opportunities to practice using academic language in authentic ways. Oral language practice helps students develop and deepen content knowledge and supports their listening, speaking, reading, and writing skills. In pairs and small groups, English learners practice new language structures and vocabulary that they have been taught. In a typical classroom, the teacher calls on one student at a time, which doesn't provide the type of language-rich environment English learners need. As discussed throughout this section, English learners benefit from opportunities to work with peers or the teacher in expressing their ideas, clarifying ideas and concepts, and gaining practice in speaking English. In Section 3, Julie shows a Log of Student Participation in Oral Activities (Figure 3–7), which is a useful way of ensuring that all students are contributing their ideas to a discussion regardless of their English proficiency level.

Practice & Application

Integrate all language skills (i.e., reading, writing, speaking, and listening) in activities so that students have ample practice with all aspects of language.

Typically, teachers present new material through lecture and neglect the opportunity for students to practice the new language and content knowledge through multiple modalities. Effective lessons include a variety of activities that encourage students to apply both the content and language skills they are learning through means such as hands-on materials, group assignments, partner work, and projects. In a fourth-grade class where 80 percent of the students were economically disadvantaged and 37.7 percent were English learners, writing was an area of focus and was practiced using a creative process. The teacher first had students draw a storyboard of their narrative and then, using the storyboard, tell the story to a peer, at which point necessary details or chronology of events were clarified. Once the stories were written, the teacher noted common errors that students made and minilessons were dedicated to teaching one specific skill at a time with lots of opportunities to practice

You'll see examples of how English learners used images to support the writing of science texts

see Section 3, page 71

and apply the skill. For instance, the class worked on using dialogue in their stories to add expression and interest. They were permitted to revise a story adding appropriate dialogue or to write a new story. The same process was used with a variety of skills such as punctuation and aspects of grammar. On the district writing test in this particular year, 56 percent of the students in this class were commended, meaning that they received a score of 3 or 4 on a 4-point scale for their composition. By comparison, only 19 percent of English learners in the district were commended and 34 percent of all students tested in the district were commended (Echevarria, Richards-Tutor, and Vogt 2015).

Lesson Delivery

Use activities and instruction that support content and language objectives and keep students engaged.

Throughout the lesson, the tasks, activities, and teaching all work together to support content and language objectives. Sometimes teachers drift away from the focus of the lesson in their discussions or the activities selected for students to complete aren't tightly related to the lesson's objectives. Unfocused teaching or unclear explanations of assignments lead to students being off-task or disengaged. Because English learners are trying to make sense of the language and content, they are more likely to be engaged in lessons that stay focused on their stated purpose. When teachers spend their time and energy teaching students the content they need to learn, students typically learn the material, but when students spend their time *actively engaged* in activities that strongly relate to the material they'll be tested on, they learn more of the material (Leinhardt, Bickel, and Pallay 1982).

Review & Assessment

Provide regular feedback to students on their output (e.g., language, content, work) so that they are aware of correct usage of language as well as clarifying misunderstandings about the lesson's content.

Teachers need to assess student comprehension and learning throughout the lesson to ensure that English learners are making consistent progress in acquisition of content and language. Frequent checks of student comprehension are used to determine whether additional explanation or reteaching is needed. By doing so, teachers can also provide feedback on correct and incorrect responses, a practice shown to benefit English learners (August and Shanahan 2006). Formative assessments, or daily ongoing monitoring of progress through observations, questioning, and informal assessments, are critical for English learners to make academic gains. Also, formative assessments help teachers gauge whether or not English learners are meeting the language objectives that are designed to develop their English language proficiency.

Summary

Teachers' expectations for English learners and their behavior toward these students make a difference, either positively or negatively. English learners cannot participate fully in academic lessons without instructional supports provided by their teachers. All students are learning rigorous content to attain high academic standards, but English learners in particular must have supports such as those discussed in this section to make content comprehensible for them. Furthermore, there needs to be a dedicated time each day for ELD as well as attention paid to language throughout the school day so that students make progress toward acquiring the academic language required for school success. With teachers who focus on academic language and put supports in place for accessing content, English learners can make significant academic progress.

SECTION 3

BUT THAT

Teaching from an Asset Perspective

JULIE NORA

Some of the world's most celebrated artists and writers—Vladimir Nabokov, Joseph Conrad, and Salvador Dali, to name only a few—know more than one language and have lived in a variety of cultures. These experiences and knowledge are assets, particularly in our globally connected world. The English learners (ELs) in the United States bring this same value into our society and our schools—their knowledge of another language and another culture can enrich the learning of all students—but too often we judge them only in terms of their limitations in the language and dominant culture they are learning (we even call them *limited English proficient*). We overlook the assets they have and fail to build on what they already know. If, as educators, we can affirm who they are, build on their strengths, and develop their academic skills and English language proficiency, we will help them be successful and develop the kinds of skills we want *all* our students to have.

Teacher-provided language-based scaffolds are essential to making this happen, but many ELs and former ELs are placed in mainstream classrooms with teachers who have little or no training in how to meet their needs. The goal of this section is to help educators support language acquisition while deepening content-area learning and access to higher-order thinking. To begin, let's consider what it means to be an "EL."

Students Are More Than "English Learners"

I recently was at a conference where Marta was presenting her experience in going to school in the United States. Marta emigrated from her native Argentina to the United States when she was ten. In Argentina, she did well in school, but, in the United States, her academic identity was suddenly different. Overwhelmed by her new identity as an immigrant EL, Marta struggled. It took her more than a year to balance her belief that she was welcome in her new country with the depression, isolation, and confusion that she felt trying to navigate a new language and culture. She was very aware that her teachers in the States did not see her in the same way her teachers in Argentina did.

Marta was able to move past the difficulties of her first years as an EL but never forgot them. She went on to become a teacher and complete her doctorate in education—focusing on ELs to no surprise! She credits her success in part to her parents. They never questioned whether Marta would go to college, believed in her ability to succeed, and knew the strengths she had as a student in Argentina. They also acknowledged the challenges she experienced in the United States. Her parents knew her and had high expectations for her.

As Jana explains in Section 2, ELs are more successful when their teachers get to know them. The reality that learning is centered in relationships is not new, and yet we often let this essential piece go. We cannot let it go for our ELs. Without knowing who our ELs are—their experiences, their strengths, their struggles, their hopes, and their needs—we can't move beyond the label of "EL" to see the students in front of us.

Any label compromises an individual student's identity. We need more information about a student than a label like "EL." Knowing Marta was an EL did not tell us that her father was college-educated, that her mother insisted on no uncertain terms that Marta would go to college, that she knew a great deal about the history of Argentina and Latin America, that she loved reading, that she had two brothers. . . . Yet this is not easy.

There is great diversity among students who come to U.S. schools not fully proficient in English. In a single classroom, a teacher might have students from several different countries who speak several different languages—or who speak the same language (Spanish, for example) but come from different countries and backgrounds (Colombia, Guatemala, Mexico, and El Salvador). Even students whose parents are from the same country of origin don't all have the same story. Many were born in the United States; some came to the States after starting school in another country and learning in another language; some may have fled war-torn areas with their families; some may have left stable environments; some may have had an uninterrupted, high-quality education; some may have had limited formal schooling. It is easy for us to make assumptions about students' experiences, which argues the need for countering that momentum by getting to know our students. We need to see how very different their experiences can be. For example, I know two students, both from Colombia. One's family members were victims of guerillas and moved to the United States as political refugees; the other's parents came seeking employment opportunities. And those are just two points of difference. I haven't said what their passions are, what kinds of relationships they have, let alone their academic identities—their relative strengths and needs relative to their ability to use language in speaking, listening, reading, and writing.

To get to know our students' strengths and needs, we need to create opportunities for them to share themselves with us. Of course, this is work we should be doing with every student, but we already know some things about students who share our cultural background. Even when we do not share the same cultural background as our students, it's not hard to learn about theirs. Ms. Thompson, a ninth-grade history teacher, has a heterogeneous classroom of native English speakers as well as ELs, one of whom is Miguel Valdéz. During the first few weeks of school, she gathers information about Miguel by looking at his records, as well as interviewing him, collecting key data about him on the information sheet in Figure 3–1.

> As Jana explained in Section 2, when positive inquiry into our students' individual strengths is part of our teaching, our teaching becomes stronger.

Ms. Thompson learns about Miguel through a variety of means. She has access to his school report records from Colombia. By looking at his academic records with a Spanish-proficient colleague from her school, she learns that he had been in school consistently grades K–5 and performed at or above grade level. An interview with his parents reveals that he was *un muy buen estudiante* (a very good student) and that he was reading and writing in Spanish at fifth-grade level when he left Colombia. She also learns that the family uses only Spanish at home. Using this variety of means to learn about Miguel gave Ms. Thompson a more complete picture of him—including his assets and needs. For example, learning that Miguel had a strong foundation in Spanish, that using Spanish with his family was an essential part of his daily life, and believing that being bilingual is an asset for any student, Ms. Thompson made it a goal to provide Miguel with the opportunity to continue to develop his Spanish skills so he would not lose this valuable asset.

Affirm Student Identity

Once Ms. Thompson learns about her students, she creates ways to affirm these identities (see Figure 3–2). For example, she creates a unit to help students understand that many different cultural groups have come to our state over the course of its history and that we each have our own reasons and stories about our family coming to Rhode Island (see Figure 3–3).

Figure 3–1 Student Information Sheet

Student	Miguel Valdéz		
Date of birth	6/19/2001		
Country of origin	Colombia		
Date arrived in U.S.	8/1/2012		
Area		**Strengths**	**Needs**	**Teaching Implications**
Native language	Spanish	Strong foundation; attended school in Colombia grades K–5	Opportunities to continue Spanish language development	Determine what he can transfer from Spanish to English
Language of instruction	English	Performed well in English-as-a-second-language classes grades 6–8; exited limited English proficient status in three years; has communicative competence in English (uses languages in social settings with peers and teachers)	Academic vocabulary for content area	Provide explicit vocabulary instruction
			More complex sentences	Provide opportunities for interaction with native language peers
			Greater variety of sentence types in both oral and written language	Teach language structures explicitly

(continues)

Figure 3–1 *(continued)*

Area	Strengths	Needs	Teaching Implications
Other languages	None		
Formal education experiences	Attended one public school grades K–5 in Colombia	Has a strong foundation in math, science, Spanish language and literacy, history of Colombia/Latin America	Background knowledge of U.S. history	Provide explicit instruction in key concepts that other students may have already learned K–5
Family information	Mother, father, and younger sister live with student; father was a physical therapist in native Colombia	Value education, attended school through university in native Colombia	Interpretation/translation in English Orientation to school practices	Parents support school and can support child in native language

Figure 3–2 Guidelines for Identity-Affirming Instruction for ELs

- Create units that integrate students' identities.

- Provide opportunities for students to speak, write, and reflect on concepts that are integral to their lives, such as immigration, their languages and cultures, and their countries of origin.

- Include important figures from students' cultures in projects and inquiries.

- Gather a classroom library of diverse texts by and about people of diverse cultures.

- Celebrate the native languages of all the students in the classroom.

As part of a social studies unit on immigration, Ms. Thompson focuses on the question, "Why do people decide to live where they do or move to other places?" (National Council for the Social Studies [NCSS] 2013, 43).

Figure 3–3 "Coming to Rhode Island" Lesson

The exhibition features the lives of four of what the museum calls "pioneers," or individuals who came to our state at the forefront of an immigration pattern. Each pioneer has an exhibition space that recreates some aspect of his or her life:

1. A young girl who came from England in the 1600s for religious reasons. The exhibition depicts part of her home.

2. A young man from Quebec who came in the 1800s to work in the mills. His exhibition features parts of a mill.

3. A man from Cape Verde who came for economic opportunities. His exhibition features a ship because he carried goods and people between Rhode Island and Cape Verde.

4. A woman who came to Rhode Island from the Dominican Republic in the 1950s in search of economic opportunity. The exhibition "Fefa's Market" features a bodega because she and her husband opened a bodega.

(continues)

Figure 3–3 *(continued)*

Students rotate between two activities: learning from an oral historian who created one of the exhibits and doing a scavenger hunt of the four pioneer exhibitions.

Activity 1: An oral historian tells her story

A local oral historian contributed to the creation of one of the exhibits through her oral history. Students learn from the oral historian about how she used the tools of oral history to learn about and document one of the pioneer's stories and the role that the pioneer played in the immigration of Dominicans. The historian brings in her tools (a tape recorder, for example) to share with the students.

Students are taught how historians learn from letters, photographs, artifacts, maps, land surveys, census information, historical documents, media, architecture, interviews and biographies, and, specifically, about the role of oral histories.

Activity 2: Coming to the Rhode Island exhibition

Teachers begin by introducing the exhibition to the students and letting all students in the group explore the timeline for five minutes. The goal is to build some prior knowledge of the exhibit's subject.

Guiding questions when the groups come back:

- What is this exhibit about?
- How are people's stories told?
- What is the timeline?

Then students are then sent off on scavenger hunts. Each group has copies of the hunts, two clipboards, and sticky notes to record what they learn.

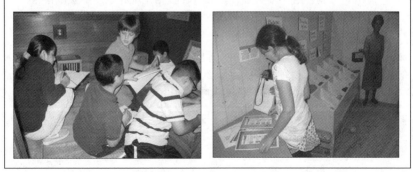

The scavenger hunts explore the following questions: Why did the pioneers come? What did they bring? What did they leave behind? How did they live? Additionally, each group explores a hunt related to just one pioneer so students become experts on that pioneer. There are written labels and visual artifacts in each exhibition where the students can read the answer to each of these questions. Students explore the exhibitions in small groups and then gather back together to share what they learned.

Students place their sticky notes on a large piece of butcher paper that lists the name of each pioneer and the questions.

	Pioneer 1	Pioneer 2	Pioneer 3	Pioneer 4
Why did he or she come?				
What did he or she bring?				
What did he or she leave behind?				
How did he or she live?				
What else did you learn about the pioneer?				

Debrief
After placing their sticky notes on the paper, students share what they learned about each of the pioneers with the other groups. They then compare the similarities and differences among the four pioneers by comparing what students learned.

Students share expertise about each of the pioneers they explored in depth with each other. The students discuss the following questions that explore the concepts involved and are asked to share one thing they discussed at the very end.

- What is culture? (Culture is how people behave, what they believe, what is important to them, what their traditions are, and how they live with others.)

(continues)

Figure 3–3 (*continued*)

- What did you learn about the different cultures of the four pioneers in the Coming to Rhode Island exhibition? (A state is occupied by people of many cultures.)

- Why do you think these four pioneers chose to live in Rhode Island? (People choose to live in different states for different reasons—for example, climate, health, industry, political persecution, geography, language and culture.)

- How did the museum curators learn about these four pioneers? (One can learn about history through letters, photographs, artifacts, maps, land surveys, census information, historical documents, media, architecture, interviews, and biographies.)

- How did you learn about pioneers' lives through this exhibition? (One can learn about history through letters, photographs, artifacts, maps, land surveys, census information, historical documents, media, architecture, interviews, and biographies.)

- How was life for each of these characters different from life today? (Promotes understanding history through concepts such as past, present, future, and similarity and change.)

Follow-up Activity: "Dear . . ."
The day after the visit, students are assigned to ask their families the following questions:

- Who is the first person from our family who lived in or came to Rhode Island?

- When did he or she live?

- Was he or she native or did he or she immigrate to Rhode Island?

- Why did he or she live in or come to Rhode Island?

- What questions would you like to ask this person?

- What would you like to tell this person about your life today?

Using a computer, students then write a letter to the first person in their family who lived in or came to Rhode Island.

From this activity, students come to understand that each of us has something in common—a family member who came to live in our state or who was indigenous to our state—and that understanding our past helps us understand our present.

Such educational experiences help establish certain foundational understandings about the culture of the United States and the larger global society: we carry identities from other places and past generations. The United States is a country of immigrants, but usually only first-generation immigrants identify as such. "EL" does not necessarily mean that a student sees herself as an immigrant. Many ELs are first- and second-generation natives to the United States and identify as their ethnicity (Latino or Chinese, for example, not "immigrant"). Ms. Thompson's lesson asks students to identify the first member of their family who came to the state in which they live to acknowledge that migration is an ongoing part of human experience. As adults, the native English and EL students in our classroom will be likely to live in another state or even another country.

Students learn the many different reasons—economic, political, educational, personal—people have for leaving one place for another. Ms. Thompson is able to draw on students' examples to connect Isaac's story of his great-grandparents leaving Russia for political reasons in the early 1900s to Miguel's parents leaving Colombia. She encourages students to invite relatives to school to share first-person stories, always following these visits with classroom discussions about connections between stories. When a family member cannot speak English, interpreters can often be found through parent organizations or paid interpreters. These invitations recognize diverse families' contributions to all students' learning.

> This is just one example of the many ways teachers can structure instruction around both content-area knowledge and skills and learning about themselves and each other.

We can invite students' identities into school in multiple other ways. At the school where my friend Lorilee Cabrera Liberato coaches, the annual Authors' Parade invites students to dress up as characters from fiction and nonfiction books they've read. In the past, there were neither characters nor authors that represented all of the students. Eighty percent of the students at this school identify as Latino, and many are

Puerto Rican. When the school launched the event this year, Lorilee looked around to see students dressed up as *jibaritos* and *jibaritas* (noble and humble mountain-dwelling peasants) for the first time. They were singing traditional songs from the island of Puerto Rico, accompanied by Afro-Puerto Rican musicians (for her own firsthand account, see www.heinemann.com/blog/fellows-lcliberato-2-1-21/). In preparation for this event, students had studied a character from folklore, Juan Bobo, a *jibarito*. Lorilee describes how one Latina teacher became emotional when she saw families and kids singing and dancing and celebrating their culture. The Latina teacher was deeply moved and described the power of seeing families, children, and their teachers together singing, dancing, and celebrating their culture: too often, children in the United States only encounter negative portrayals of Puerto Ricans. School librarians and teachers can not only collect materials that celebrate children's culture, but use them in meaningful ways, as in this example.

Colleagues and families can also be resources for learning. For example, the suggestion to create an Authors' Parade based on individual children's characters from the *jibarito* study came from a Latina teacher in Lorilee's school. Administrators and teachers have tremendous resources in their peers and can benefit from soliciting ideas of how to incorporate culturally relevant learning into their teaching. Ms. Thompson, Miguel's teacher, invited Miguel's father to join the school's health and wellness committee after she learned that he was a licensed physical therapist in Colombia (recall Figure 3–1) who is unable to practice in the United States. Because Mr. Valdez is still learning English, another committee member who speaks Spanish interprets for him during meetings. Soon, he took the initiative to organize an annual walk in a nearby state park, plotting the trail with chalk and leading students and their families on the walk. We can only recognize the assets in our community when we have an asset perspective.

Learning Is Language-Based

It is essential to affirm student identity, but it is not enough. Amid all this work, it's important to remind ourselves that learning happens primarily through language for all students (not just ELs). We use language to make meaning of the world around us. Language—either spoken or written—allows us to probe for specificity, deepen and communicate our understanding, and, in doing so, advance collective understanding. We must learn the language required to participate in our community. In school, students must learn the social language that allows them to interact with their peers and teachers, as well as the academic language that allows them to develop their understanding of grade-level content. Without this language, learning is limited.

As educators, we must appreciate the extent of the language demands of school. For example, in the lesson in Figure 3–4 students are asked to listen, write, read, and speak. Each activity is a vehicle for accessing and sharing knowledge and thinking. To be successful,

Figure 3–4 Grade 8 History Lesson on the Settlement of the Great Plains After the Civil War

---

Teacher: "What would it be like to settle in a remote location? What might your surroundings be like? What might you need to survive? Write a response in your journals."

After the students have completed their responses, they share their ideas during a class discussion.

The teacher then distributes a text describing the features of the Great Plains. The students read the text and create a T-chart comparing the features of the remote location they described with those of the Great Plains.

Next, pairs of students describe the challenges that existed for those seeking to settle the Great Plains after the Civil War and list the technological tools the settlers might have needed.

After approximately fifteen minutes, each pair shares what they discussed with the whole group.

---

learners need to understand domain-specific vocabulary and genres. Through language, students activate prior knowledge, compare and contrast, clarify their understanding, and apply new knowledge. These tasks are much more complicated for students who are learning English.

Value and Build on Students' Native Languages

All ELs by definition speak a language other than English. There are several reasons we should value the use of these languages. First, it is often the language that students use at home with their families. Language and identity are intertwined. Teachers who acknowledge and value their students' languages are essentially acknowledging and valuing the identities and lives of their students. This is key in developing relationships and trust. Encouraging students to use their native languages also facilitates their learning: sometimes ELs rely on what they already know—their native language—when they do not know the language of instruction. As Jana illustrates in Section 2, when students are able to use their home language and English in school, they perform on levels similar to their English-speaking peers. They also come to value their home language as a resource in our globally connected world where being multilingual is a benefit.

> Consider how much is lost in the "English-only" policy still in place in many classrooms and schools.

Valuing our students' native languages can be done in many ways. First, we need to find out what those languages are. Just asking sends a powerful message. Then, we must communicate explicitly that we see students' native languages as resources, not deficits, and that we value multilingualism. We could create and display a chart of all the languages spoken by students and their families and discuss the languages of the historical figures, mathematicians, scientists, and so on that students encounter in their lessons.

We also need to allow students to use their native language to develop content knowledge, either by speaking with peers or reading.

In an English-language classroom the end goal is for students to use English, but this should not be at the expense of their native language and will be facilitated through access to complex concepts in a language they understand.

If students use a phrase in their native language when talking or writing in English, we should help them translate. During a science unit, Mr. Barnes has his kindergartners watch a chick hatch. He confers with Elisa to learn what she knows and to give her the opportunity to use academic language with his support. First he asks Elisa to describe what happened when the chicks hatched. She says, "*Primeiro*, a little hole." Instead of immediately elaborating himself, Mr. Barnes encourages Elisa to do so by asking questions that require more than a one-word answer: "What else? Say more." Eventually, he restates what Elisa says using her mix of native Portuguese and limited English in more elaborate academic language: "First the chick made a hole in the shell?" He listens carefully and records not only the concepts that Elisa understands but also her language capacities and needs, so he can adjust his instruction. Because several students need to develop process vocabulary (*first, second, third*), Mr. Barnes subsequently presents a minilesson to the whole class. He then holds the students accountable for using that language in subsequent lessons that involve steps.

Note that Mr. Barnes doesn't tell Elisa she is using the wrong word (*primeiro*, the Portuguese word for *first*) when he is assessing her knowledge of the stages of the hatching of a chick. Instead, he includes it in his notes and then decides to teach process words in English for a group of students who also do not use these words. Because Elisa understands the concept and knows how to say *first, second, third* in Portuguese but not in English, he helps her make a list of process words in Portuguese with their English equivalents next to them (see Figure 3–5), thereby acknowledging and celebrating her understanding of the concept.

Figure 3–5 Elisa's List of Process Words

	Portuguese	**English**
1st	primeiro	first
2nd	segundo	second
3rd	terceiro	third
4th	quarto	fourth

Not all of us are proficient in the languages of our students, but if we can gain a minimal understanding of their languages, we can build on our students' existing strengths. For example, Ms. Thompson teaches English and Spanish cognates (see Figure 3–6) to help the Spanish speakers in her classroom connect the two languages.

Figure 3–6 English and Spanish Cognates

Cognates/Cognados	
English	español
geography	geografía
map	mapa
longitude	longitude
latitude	latitud
immigration	imigración
emigration	emigración

She tells students that cognates are words in two languages that have the same origin, and that being aware of cognates between Spanish and English will help them learn English. She has her students keep a log of cognates they come across when speaking or reading. From time to time she presents a minilesson to a small group of Spanish speakers about the cognates' similarities and differences (that the *-tion* ending in English is *-ción* in Spanish, for example). By asking her EL teacher or Spanish teacher for advice on challenges learning English, she learns that this particular family of cognates can cause problems for Spanish speakers learning to speak English because of different stress patterns in the two languages. She therefore makes sure that not only can these students read and write words with this suffix, but that they can hear and say it.

In her cognate chart, Ms. Thompson writes *English* and *español* and *cognate* and *cognados* and lists words in both languages, sending a clear message that having more than one language in her classroom is valued. She allows students who speak the same language to use their native language in the classroom, encourages them to interpret for one another if they can, and tries to learn and use words from the languages of her students. At the beginning of each year, she makes a list of all of the languages of her students and proudly posts them in her class. She never punishes students for using their native language.

Of course, we don't have the time or capacity to learn all the native languages spoken in a classroom or a school, but using a few content-area words in a new student's native language and considering how to strategically build bridges between native language and English is worth the effort. (The school's EL support staff may be able to help and, if not, there are many translation apps that can aid communication.) When students feel validated, they are more willing to take risks and participate, which in turn helps them grow and develop. Creating a safe classroom community by having an asset orientation toward students, getting to know them, and affirming their culture and native language creates a strong foundation.

Although some ELs will arrive at schools with strong native language skills, some ELs may have limited skills in English and in their native language. For example, I recall Luis, a fifth-grade EL who had attended school in Puerto Rico in Spanish for kindergarten and then came to the States when he was in first grade, at which time he began learning only in English. He continued to use Spanish with his family and friends but never had the opportunity to develop academic or complex native language skills in Spanish and was still in the process of developing academic language in English. Students such as Luis will not be able to transfer their knowledge and skills from their native language. They need help to develop academic language in English. A colleague, Ms. Carson, was especially gifted at helping her students do this. She knew that many of her students had not been exposed to the academic vocabulary they needed to understand the concepts that she was teaching. She told me that in the past she had tried to give students lists of the important words and their definitions to memorize, but that this practice did not lead to their learning the vocabulary. Then she started teaching vocabulary in a different way. She would introduce new vocabulary by using the new term herself in class. Sometimes she would provide students with a drawing or image that represented the word. She then had her students draw a picture that represented the word. Next she gave students the opportunity to use and to discuss the vocabulary with their peers. She found that when she spent this time giving students the opportunity to not only be told the meaning of the academic vocabulary, but also to use and discuss it, her students were able to comprehend the content of her lessons more thoroughly. They were then able to begin using the new words in their oral and written language.

Model and Create Opportunities to Use Academic Language

Using and learning language are interactive processes. For some ELs, school is the only place they are exposed to academic English. By intentionally facilitating ELs' interaction with academic English, we expedite their development of language and their learning. Teachers are in an ideal position to model language. We can modify academic English so that ELs can understand and explicitly learn the language structures. We need to simplify our language (without dumbing it down), avoid idiomatic expressions, and speak clearly—with enunciation and not too fast or too slowly.

We must help ELs develop the language they need to socialize and be successful in school. When I moved from my native California and began teaching in a Rhode Island middle school, I was surprised that some of my advanced English-learning students not only were fully communicative in English—that is they could carry on a conversation with me easily—but also had local accents. Many ELs learn social language—the contextualized language used in everyday communication—more quickly than they learn academic language, which is abstract and more complex. Like my middle school students, they may pick up social language but must be explicitly exposed to and taught academic language.

In Section 2, Jana cites research (Cummins 1981) suggesting that even when students are orally proficient in English, they likely have not acquired the academic language to access learning at the level of their native English-speaking peers. This is because acquiring academic language is a more complex process than acquiring social language. When we don't provide scaffolds for students who are not native speakers of English, many of their actions often mimic what's expected without achieving it. Impersonating the physical behavior of a reader is not reading. Too often ELs learn to "play school"—sit, be quiet, follow orders—but don't become as knowledgeable or as proficient as their non-EL peers. In Section 2, Jana lists the multitude of skills required just in the Common Core State Standards. Understanding academic English is essential to being successful in school. When students cannot fully comprehend, speak, read, or write the language of school, they need particular supports to develop their academic English language proficiency so that they can access content and higher-order thinking. ELs should not be allowed to remain silent and invisible.

As an administrator of an elementary school, I spend part of every day in the cafeteria. Students ask me for permission for a variety of things—to use the bathroom, to get a drink of water, to go see the nurse. There is a pattern in the language of their questions. When asking to use the restroom or get a drink of water, they simply ask for permission. However, when they ask to go to the nurse, they include the reason (often a very elaborate one!). Now, I rarely deny a child permission to go to the nurse and don't expect them to provide a justification. They do so because their classroom teachers—rightly—must know if they need to be escorted, are going to be sick on the way, and so on. The children have internalized this expectation and modified their language to accommodate it.

All students are also motivated by interaction with their peers. The Practice Guide, "Effective Literacy and English Language Instruction for English Learners in Elementary Grades" (Gersten et al. 2007) recommends that teachers provide ELs with about ninety minutes per week of opportunities to partner with students with varying levels of English proficiency in structured, academic tasks that are connected to what they are learning. We should therefore facilitate opportunities for ELs to interact with their native English-speaking classmates. Many teachers of English-proficient students use cooperative learning. This is challenging for ELs because they may not have the same level of language skills, but we can still use cooperative learning if we preteach the language students will need to use with one another, provide scaffolds, and carefully consider student groupings.

Depending on our ELs' language level, we can model the language required to participate in a cooperative group and support them as they practice it. We can provide sentence prompts, vocabulary lists, and visual supports, and give them opportunities to practice the language in pairs before having them do so in larger cooperative groups. We must always be explicit about the norms of participation, which could include contributing ideas, listening to classmates, and staying on task. ELs may not be accustomed to these participant structures.

Although they may not be able to express their thoughts in ways that are as complex as their native English-speaking peers, their thinking may be as complex or more so. It is therefore essential to engage them in conversations to draw out their thinking and teach explicitly the language structures they need in order to participate. We need to make sure all students feel comfortable contributing regardless of their level of language development. We also need to give feedback not only on the content of the cooperative exchanges but also on the participation of all members and how each follows participation norms. One way is to have students complete a rubric based on the norms we have created.

Mr. Thomas leads his second graders in an inquiry-based science unit on insects. Over the course of the unit, students will use evidence to create a scientific explanation about how insects depend on their habitat. They will analyze and interpret data on the nonliving elements of a habitat, evaluate and give feedback on other scientific explanations of why insects can survive in their habitats, determine how insects depend on the health of their habitats, collaborate with others to explain how organisms depend on their habitat, and analyze and interpret data about the structures and behaviors of insects that help them survive. First, Mr. Thomas finds out what his students already know about milkweed bugs. He places an image of a milkweed bug in the middle of a web graphic organizer and asks students to write everything they know about the milkweed bug.

Realizing that his second graders need to know vocabulary related to insect parts (*head, thorax, abdomen*) and key structures of insects and their functions (*antenna, eye, mouth, wings, legs, exoskeleton*), Mr. Thomas then introduces the key vocabulary (*head, thorax, abdomen, antenna, eye, mouth, wings, legs, exoskeleton*) and has students label a diagram to have as a resource. He reinforces this vocabulary by taking a "picture walk" through a book on the life cycle of a milkweed bug. Students label the body parts, but Mr. Thomas' teaching doesn't end there. He takes the next step, asking students why they think each structure will help the milkweed bug survive. The students talk in pairs and small groups that have similar language expectations. He observes these groups and speaks with students individually to determine whether they are learning the concepts as well as the appropriate language, and then designs subsequent interventions. By introducing key vocabulary, he is setting the students up to be successful in completing the other academic tasks that will involve understanding and using the academic vocabulary.

Provide Feedback That Recognizes Approximation

When students don't answer a question or respond to a writing assignment, we sometimes think they can't or don't want to. This is often untrue. I recently observed a class of ELs whom I knew quite well. The teacher, Ms. Cole, asked the entire class, "What is the Constitution?" and called on Juana to respond. She and I knew Juana knew the answer, yet Juana refused to speak. Ms. Cole quickly had the students turn and talk to a neighbor, lowering the stakes: students didn't have to speak in front of the whole class but rather to each other. She then asked the students to write what they discussed with their partner on a piece of chart paper. Afterward, I asked Juana why she was hesitant to speak in the whole-class setting. She said she was embarrassed that she might mispronounce a word or respond in the "wrong way." She was unable to own her mastery of the content because of her uncertainty with language. What could have been a moment of celebration was instead a moment of private shame and fear.

How often does this happen for the ELs in our classes? We can't know, but we can take steps to ensure that making mistakes is not a cause for shame. If infants learning to talk were shamed for their approximations (saying *baba* instead of *bottle*, for example), would they be motivated to continue attempting to talk? Juana had not been shamed by her teacher, but she hadn't yet seen enough examples of supported risk-taking, such as students like herself speaking in incomplete utterances in front of the whole class. Until she does, she'll choose silence in the whole-class setting.

When we don't demonstrate that we value approximations, we unintentionally silence our students. Supporting risk-taking is not just limited to how we structure classroom talk, of course, but to all forms of participation: listening, writing, reading, and speaking.

Here's another example of how we can provide supportive feedback. A teacher asked students to name the three branches of government. One student knew the three branches but was nervous about saying these multisyllabic words in front of the entire class. When he tentatively began, "Le . . . ," the teacher asked, "Legislative?" This gave the student the power to confirm or correct the prompt and to practice saying the word. With a smile, he nodded and pronounced the full word, "Legislative."

In 2003, I was observing an eighth-grade social studies class discuss the powers of the U.S. presidency. The teacher brought up the then-current U.S. war with Iraq: "There has been talk that this war is going to be really quick. Do you think it will take more than a year? Imagine it does take more than a year. Will that hurt the President or help him?" An EL responded, "Too much people are dying." At first glance it is clear that the student used incorrect grammar and it might appear that the student is not answering the question directly. Recognizing what the student was implying, the teacher restated the answer with an elaborated, grammatically correct response: "So, you think it will hurt the President if the war goes on for more than a year because more people will die and the voters will not like that?" The student nodded in agreement.

When students are still learning language, they may not be able to express their thinking fully. We must be especially attentive to recognizing when a student's response implies a viable understanding of the concept being discussed. Also, when students use incorrect grammar or pronunciation in an oral response, focusing on it makes them self-conscious about their speaking, diverts them from thinking about the content, and discourages them from participating. Instead of correcting students overtly, we should provide examples of academic language by restating what the students said. This allows them to participate more actively, feel comfortable using oral language, and develop their language skills.

When a student . . .	Instead of . . .	Do this . . .
Uses an incorrect grammatical form	Explicitly pointing out the grammatical error	Restate the student's statement using the correct form
Gives a limited response	Saying, "No, that is wrong"	Elaborate on the student's response
Says something you do not understand	Ignoring it	Ask for clarification
Does not respond immediately	Going on to other students	Give adequate wait time

Use Wait Time

Another way we can encourage risk-taking and student participation is through wait, or think, time—the period of silence after we ask a question before a student responds. Sometimes we feel uncomfortable with silence and too quickly call on a student who has raised a hand or we answer the question ourselves. However, providing all students with adequate time to process relevant information increases students' responses and enriches our questioning strategies. By waiting in silence, often longer than it feels comfortable for a teacher, and demanding respect for such silences, we create more opportunities for students to think, generate responses, and use oral language. ELs in particular understand more than they can articulate, especially in the beginning stages of learning the language. They need more time to process information. The amount and quality of their spoken or written language is also more limited, less complex. We sometimes think ELs who do not voluntarily contribute orally or who give one-word answers don't understand the discussion or don't have anything to contribute. We need to give ELs enough time to respond to the questions they are asked and let students know we expect everyone to be involved.

Here is an example. Students in a high school social studies class are learning about urban growth in the United States. Their teacher wants to activate their prior knowledge of cities. She knows Maria previously lived in Chicago and has much to share about the aspects of a big city—population density, traffic congestion, public transportation, architecture, and so on. She also knows that Maria will need more time to process the question and formulate her response than her native English-speaking peers. She uses two strategies to help give Maria the time she needs.

First, she encourages all the students to take time to formulate their thoughts: "I am going to ask you a question. But I am going to wait a full minute before I call on anyone, so do not raise your hand until I tell you that the minute is up. Here is the question, 'What do you already know about cities?'" She writes *What do you already know about cities?* on the board as a visual reference and textual support. "Feel free to write down any notes. Remember, do not raise your hand until I tell you to." After one minute, she says, "If you are ready to share something you know about cities, raise your hand." Although Maria does not raise her hand, the teacher has noticed her taking many notes, so she says, "I am going to give you thirty more seconds. Those of you who are ready, think of anything else you know about cities. Those of you who did not raise your hand have thirty more seconds to formulate your response. Continue making notes about what you already know about cities." After thirty seconds, she again asks who is ready. This time Maria raises her hand, and the teacher calls on her.

When Maria does not speak immediately, the teacher uses the second strategy: she waits five seconds, counting in her head to force herself to wait longer than she's comfortable doing. Before she gets to five, Maria begins: "Many peoples live there. There are many cars and buses to move people. It takes a long time to go to work. There is a lot of pollution."

By giving all students time to formulate their thoughts and responses and allowing adequate wait time, this teacher made it possible for Maria to share what she knew about cities and participate in the whole-group discussion. Wanting to reinforce how important it is for students to explore and formulate their thoughts before responding, the teacher concludes by saying, "I love how you all took your time to consider your response carefully and wrote it down so you could remember before responding. You gave thoughtful responses as a result."

Create a Safe Classroom Environment That Values Risk-Taking

Fourth-grade teacher Ms. Wollman has a class of native English speakers and ELs. She knows her ELs might not be as willing to speak up in whole-group settings, maybe not even when paired with a native speaker, for fear of being made fun of because of their developing English. When she and her students establish their classroom rules at the beginning of the year, she includes a rule that validates taking risks—"Take risks and make misteaks"—then points out the mistake in her rule as an example of how we are all learning, even she.

Another strategy is to write questions on pieces of paper, give one to each student, and allow the students to write their responses. We can vary the complexity of the questions and distribute them based on students' present performance levels, calling on students once we see that they have had the chance to formulate a response. Alternatively, we can have students write their own questions individually or with a peer, have them formulate answers to their questions, and share either as a pair or with the whole class.

Think-Pair-Share and Turn and Talk

Another way that teachers can give students opportunities to formulate their ideas, discuss them in a safe space, and thereby develop their oral language and vocabulary, is by having them talk with a peer through strategies such as *think-pair-share* and *turn and talk*. Mr. Thomas, the second-grade teacher who taught the science inquiry unit on insects, uses think-pair-share frequently. First, he explains what students will do when they use think-pair-share: "You will first *think* individually about a topic I present for one to three minutes. Next you will *pair* with a partner to discuss the topic. Then you and your partner will *pair* with another set of partners, and finally you will *share* what you discussed with the whole class." Then, before asking students to use the strategy, he models this with another student and answers any clarifying questions. There is an anchor chart hanging in his room featuring photos of his students, with the think-pair-share strategy summarized for students to refer to:

 think

 pair

 share

Mr. Thomas also uses *turn and talk*. As he does with think-pair-share, he introduces and models turn and talk to students before asking them to use it. He instructs them to *turn* and face their partner, have one partner *talk* about a topic the teacher has introduced while the other partner listens, and then switch so the other partner can talk. Both think-pair-share and turn and talk provide students with opportunities to develop oral language. If a teacher has a class of twenty students and the only use of oral language is between the teacher and individual students, he will be limiting the amount of time individual students use language. Both think-pair-share and turn and talk provide opportunities for ten students at a time in a class of twenty to be talking instead of just one in an exchange between the teacher and one student. Additionally, speaking to the teacher in front of the entire class can be intimidating, whereas speaking to a peer is less intimidating. As Jana points out in Section 2, oral language practice helps students develop and deepen content knowledge. In addition to helping students develop their oral language, these strategies also provide students with opportunities to develop their knowledge about a topic.

Teach Self-Advocacy

ELs may also not understand the questions they are asked. We need to encourage students to ask for clarification when they do not understand, not allow them to sit silently. We need to introduce, model, and refer to these norms at the beginning of the school year. For example:

- I will contribute my ideas.
- If I do not understand, I will let someone know.
- I will help others when I can.

We must then provide positive reinforcement when a student follows these norms: "I love how you let me know that you did not understand." Depending on how many students need this support, we might also, on an anchor chart or a sheet given to an individual student, post sentence starters and questions for students to refer to: "Can you repeat what you just said?" "I did not understand the question." "Can you ask me again in a different way?"

For example, a teacher in a high school biology class asks an EL, "Should the classification of living things be based on their genetic similarities or their morphology? Why?" A higher-level question like this, which asks students to think critically and defend their positions, should be directed to all students but *especially* to ELs, who are often asked lower-level questions. This student does not understand what is being asked of him, but instead of sitting silently and waiting for the teacher to move on to someone else, he says, "I did not understand the question." The teacher responds to his self-advocacy by saying, "Great, let's see if this helps," then writes the question on the board, provides an explicit example of the genetic similarities and morphology of two living beings, asks the question again, and the student is then able to respond.

In a third-grade classroom I observed, the teacher had the students use hand symbols to indicate they did not understand. She could then recognize when something needed clarification and either approach the student or explain in a different way for the whole class.

By allowing students to feel comfortable asking for help, we create an environment that encourages participation, higher-order thinking, and academic language. Self-advocacy is a critical tool students need to achieve their goals, become self-sufficient, and be successful in school and in life. Some ELs come from cultures in which students play a more passive role than they do in the United States. Therefore, we must teach the tools of self-advocacy.

Establish and Monitor Language Expectations

A supportive context for learning and using strategies to promote risk-taking and participation is essential but does not ensure that ELs will grow cognitively and develop academic language skills. We must expect all students to use oral language. Because ELs may be reluctant to do so, we need to not only ensure that they feel comfortable but also make sure it is happening by tracking their participation (see Figure 3–7).

Figure 3–7 Log of Student Participation in Oral Activities

Log of Student Participation in Oral Activities Date: _____ Topic: _____			
Student name	**Responds to teacher requests**	**Participates in group discussion**	**Participates in paired discussion**
Claudia	✔	✔	✔
Ahmet	✔		
Jean		✔	✔

We may permit ELs to respond in less complex ways than native speakers might, but allowing them to use minimal responses indefinitely can limit their language development. We must assess what our students can produce and then provide targeted language development activities that will expand their repertoire. Existing resources include Engage New York's language arts progressions (https://www .engageny.org/resource/new-york-state-bilingual-common-core-ini tiative) and WIDA's English Language Proficiency Standards (https:// www.wida.us/downloadLibrary.aspx), and TESOL's ESL Standards. Figure 3–8 is a portion of WIDA English Language Development Standard 5: The Language of Social Studies related to reading. There are rubrics for speaking, listening, and writing as well. These rubrics can be used to assess where a student is in the progression of language acquisition in all four areas.

Figure 3–8 WIDA Development Standard

EXPANDED STRANDS

GRADE 7

In the expanded strand that follows, students engage in analytical reading of print or digital texts to support their interpretation and ultimately, creation of charts or maps about agriculture. In order for students at all levels to maintain the same cognitive function of analyzing, educators need to ensure that students are asked to differentiate agricultural products from other resources such as mineral or human resources. This example activity consists of many parts that are not all illustrated here, including the use of the other language domains of speaking, listening, and/or writing. Language activities are almost always integrated across multiple domains in this way, and students are often asked to produce language to indicate their reading comprehension. In other words, we can't see whether students have correctly identified language or drawn conclusions based on their reading unless they show their learning in other ways. This expanded strand suggests that students would read text like that which appears next to Linguistic Complexity, but then might indicate their understanding by creating a unique chart or map. The rows for Language Forms and Conventions and Vocabulary Usage suggest some possible language learning opportunities to introduce and practice with students at each level of language proficiency. Such practice will enhance and expand students' abilities to access criteria presented through written tests.

ELD STANDARD 5: The Language of Social Studies

EXAMPLE TOPIC: Agriculture

CONNECTION: Common Core Reading Standards for Literacy in History/Social Studies, Integration of Knowledge & Ideas #7: Integrate visual information (e.g., in charts, graphs, photographs, videos, or maps) with other information in print and digital texts.

EXAMPLE CONTEXT FOR LANGUAGE USE: Students read informational text and related websites about crops or agricultural products to interpret maps or create charts.

Cognitive Function: Students at all levels of English language proficiency ANALYZE the importance of agricultural resources to regional economies.

	Level 1 Entering	Level 2 Emerging	Level 3 Developing	Level 4 Expanding	Level 5 Bridging	LEVEL 6—REACHING
READING	Identify agricultural icons using visual or graphic supports (e.g., on maps or graphs)	Locate resources or agricultural products using visual or graphic supports	Distinguish among resources or agricultural products using visual or graphic supports	Find patterns associated with resources or agricultural products using visual or graphic supports	Draw conclusions about resources or agricultural products on maps or graphs from grade-level text	

TOPIC-RELATED LANGUAGE: Students at all levels of English language proficiency interact with grade-level words and expressions, such as renewable, nonrenewable, resource allocation

We must also be aware of the cognitive level of our students' responses and consistently push them to engage in higher-order thinking. When students respond using a low-level thinking process such as recall, we should acknowledge its correctness but follow up with a prompt to use higher-level thinking. For example:

Teacher: How does a plant reproduce?
Student: The sun.
Teacher: That is correct. Tell me more about what you know about the sun and the process of photosynthesis.

Or:

Teacher: What do the actions or words of the character tell you about the character?
Student: He says, "The mountain he climbed is big."
Teacher: That's right! What does that tell you about the character?

To make sure all students have opportunities to use language and learn fully, we need to plan student participation activities carefully. Students have varying levels of oral language proficiency, and, as we have already discussed, some will be less willing to volunteer as a result. When conducting our lessons, we need to call on all students with equal regularity. ELs unaccustomed to classroom participation may need to be taught how to participate. We also need to include a variety of participation structures, such as whole class, one on one, pairs, small groups, and so on, and monitor student participation over time. For example, we could begin with a presentation in which we help students understand key concepts and vocabulary, modeling the ways we expect students to use language. If we expect them to make hypothesis statements for a science lesson, we should model making such a statement, then have students work in pairs. We can hold students accountable for participation by giving them a self- or peer-evaluation rubric and/or requiring them to record their participation.

High Expectations Through Access to Grade-Level Content

Another barrier to ELs' education is limited expectations. In an elementary school, a student newly arrived from Brazil was pulled out of his third-grade classroom to work with an English-as-a-second-language teacher during math and science. While his classmates were learning mathematical and scientific concepts, he was learning basic social language. When I asked when this student would learn math and science, the teacher said he needed to be able to communicate first. Practices like these cause ELs to fall behind their peers, but it doesn't have to be that way. We can provide ELs access to grade-level content, holding them to the same high expectations for content learning as their native-speaking peers, while providing them with the language supports they need to access new concepts.

Build Background Knowledge

ELs may lack background knowledge on grade-level content that was not covered in their countries of origin (the U.S. Constitution, for example), that they missed when they were in English-as-a-second-language programs, or that simply were not offered in elementary school—such as science as social studies—because of the increased focus on literacy and math due to high-stakes assessments. Learning what they know and building background knowledge are therefore essential. There are a variety of strategies for building background knowledge (see Figure 3–9).

Figure 3–9 Strategies for Building Background Knowledge

Use images.
Use videos.
Use graphs.
Use drawings.
Use charts.
Use maps.
Allow students to share their prior knowledge in their native language.

Here's an example of a teacher providing her ELs access to grade-level content. A class of third graders is exploring the similarities and differences in urban, rural, and suburban communities throughout the world as part of their social studies curriculum based on the College, Career, and Civic Life (C3) Framework for Social Studies State Standards. The teacher has the same goals for her ELs as she does for her English-dominant students.

The teacher conducts an initial assessment to determine what students know about rural and urban communities. Based on the information she gathers, as well as the initial assessment she has done, she realizes that not all students have the necessary background knowledge. Some are familiar with large, urban cities and others are familiar with small, rural towns.

Her goal is to compare an urban and rural community, which will fulfill one of the NCSS standards under the people, places, and environment theme:

> The study of people, places, and environments enables us to understand the relationship between human populations and the physical world. Students learn where people and places are located and why they are there. They examine the influence of physical systems, such as climate, weather, and seasons, and natural resources, such as land and water, on human populations. They study the causes, patterns, and effects of human settlement and migration, learn of the roles of different kinds of population centers in a society, and investigate the impact of human activities on the environment. This enables them to acquire a useful basis of knowledge for informed decision-making on issues arising from human-environmental relationships. (www.socialstudies.org)

Knowing that not all her students have been in or studied these types of communities, she decides to build background knowledge by showing aerial images and video clips of a rural and an urban community. She does not lead with text. The images and video clips constitute concrete examples of the two types of communities that she wants the students to compare, making the respective concepts—population density, for example—comprehensible to students even if they do not have grade-level language skills. She purposefully chooses an urban community near where the school is located and a rural community in a country one of her students is from, thereby tapping into and valuing his prior knowledge and motivating him to participate. As the students watch the videos and look at the images, they describe the characteristics of each type of community, thus using oral language with their peers.

Another strategy is to have students create something visual and then attach language and academic concepts to it (see Figure 3–10). The art teacher in my elementary school had students create two- and three-dimensional robots and label the number and types of shapes used to form each robot. Third graders exploring the concept of a food chain created a collage, identifying the primary and subsequent sources.

Figure 3–10 Visual Explanations for Academic Concepts

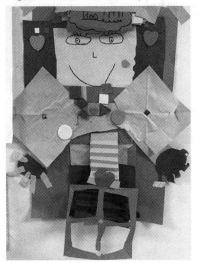

ROBOTS!

The name of my robot is _Boo Masr_

Shaa and Shemr .

My robot was designed to _care_

halloween .

My robot has ___2___ circles. ⭕
My robot has _17_ squares. ◻
My robot has ___2___ ovals. ⬭
My robot has _BXX_ rectangles. ▭
My robot has ___4___ triangles. △
My robot has ___9___ hearts. ♡

(continues)

Figure 3–10 (continued)

My Food Chain

Word	Sketch
Sun (Producer)	
Algae	
Shrimp	
Salmon	
Shark (Top Predator)	

Food Chains
A food chain is the sequence of who eats whom in an ecosystem to obtain nutrition. A food chain starts with the primary energy source, usually the sun.

My Food Chain

Word	Sketch
Sun (Producer)	pss! you could lift up my small penguin
Sun	
plankton	
Fish	
Penguin (Top Predator)	

It is also important to realize that ELs may have prior knowledge about a topic, but may not be able to share what they know because they are developing their English. By allowing students to access their prior knowledge in their native language, writing what they know or talking about it with a peer in their native language before learning about a concept or topic in English, teachers can allow them to activate their prior knowledge.

Teach Thinking Strategies

Teachers can make their high expectations clear by explicitly teaching students how to use thinking strategies. As part of her literacy instruction, Ms. Suzuki introduces and models the thinking strategy of inferring. She incorporates this strategy into her social studies unit, asking students not merely to describe what they see, but also to infer (Keene 2012). She models this strategy, has students practice the key phrases chorally, and provides sentence strips (I see . . . , I know . . . , I infer . . .) for reference. After students have an opportunity to work independently and in groups to document what they know, see, and infer, they share their inferences with a partner. She then holds an "open forum" to share how students used strategies. For example, Julian, a student in Ms. Suzuki's class, observed a helicopter landing pad in an aerial view of São Paolo, Brazil. He shared: "I saw many circles with crosses. I know they use these for *helicopteros*. I infer that there are many *helicopteros* in São Paolo." Julian then asks if another student would like to share and calls on one who volunteers. This continues until all students have shared how they used the strategy of inferring. Ms. Suzuki has established the expectation that all students will participate and holds them to it. Ms. Suzuki is giving students the opportunity to engage in higher-order thinking (inferring) and connecting it to social studies, while giving students the opportunity to develop language.

She also formatively assesses students. She uses a simple chart to keep track of whether students are using the strategy, understanding the content, and using academic language (see Figure 3–11).

Her formative assessment guides her subsequent instruction. She decides to conference with Julian individually to teach him the cognate of *helicopter* and to teach the whole class academic words such as *population*.

I am fortunate to be the leader of a dual language school where high expectations and an asset orientation toward all language learners are the norm. In our Spanish-English strand, we have native English speakers learning alongside native speakers of Spanish. The students

Figure 3–11 Assessing Strategy Use

Student	Uses inferring strategy (I see, I know, I infer)	Can describe similarities and differences between urban, rural, and suburban	Language	Goal
Susana	✔	Not yet	Uses verbs *infer*, *see*, and *know* correctly. Uses simple sentences correctly.	Use more complex sentence structures.
Julian	✔	✔	Uses verbs *infer*, *see*, and *know* correctly. Uses a word in native language: *helicopteros*.	Learn cognate of *helicopter*.
Tomas	No, describes only what he sees	✔	Uses verbs *infer*, *see*, and *know* correctly. Uses limited vocabulary.	Replace common words with academic vocabulary ("many people" with "large population").

learn grade level content in both Spanish and English. For the time that students are learning in Spanish, native Spanish-speaking students are able to share their asset, their language skills, and serve as models for the students who are learning Spanish. The same is true for English-speaking students during English time. Too often speakers of languages other than English are seen for what they cannot do— use grade-level English—not for what they can do. The dual language model is structured in such a way that these students can be seen for their assets. I will never forget what one mom of an English-speaking student said at her son's fifth-grade graduation. She described how when Josh was in second grade he began to complain about how difficult it was to learn in Spanish, that he did not understand everything. She wondered whether she should take him out of our dual language school. She didn't. And at his end-of-fifth-grade parent-teacher conference, the only concern that the Spanish side teacher had was that Josh was talking too much. The audience chuckled when Mom said, "As long as it is in Spanish, I don't care!" More importantly, she said that by being in a dual language program and learning another language and about other cultures, Josh gained empathy in a way that he could not have otherwise and that she was grateful that he did. Josh admired his Spanish-speaking peers and learned from them.

Although not all programs are dual language programs, the underlying concept of having an asset orientation toward students can be implemented in any setting, including those where students are taught entirely in English. We need to appreciate that, like Josh, students who are learning in a language that is not their native language feel uncomfortable and do not understand in the same way that native-speaking students do.

Although it takes planning and knowledge, we need to provide ELs with access to higher-order thinking and grade-level content by scaffolding instruction to make concepts understandable while also helping students develop English language proficiency. When we do this, we will help ELs be successful and reach their potential. This is important for them and for us as a society. Inequities in education have a ripple effect. Students who do not have quality educational experiences may not graduate from high school and rarely pursue postsecondary education, and we as a society are losing their potential.

AFTERWORD

NELL K. DUKE

I work at the University of Michigan, a widely respected institution that some call "the Harvard of the Midwest." In this world, the ability to speak multiple languages is highly prized. Professors who can speak multiple languages are seen capitalizing on these skills to form research and entrepreneurial collaborations, to read and translate literature from across the globe, to lead enviable study abroad trips, and to effectively communicate with a broad range of patients and clients. Indeed, all undergraduates at the university are required to take at least two years of a foreign language, with the largest college within the university strongly encouraging four years. They justify the language requirement as follows:

> [Our] language requirement seeks to prepare students for a world that has been profoundly transformed by the forces of globalization. Language shapes both how we understand and how we negotiate our world; learning a second language provides both a deep awareness of differences (linguistic and cultural) and a means to bridge them. Informed respect for other cultures, tolerance, cosmopolitanism, self-awareness, and flexibility are the hallmarks of a liberal education, and the study of foreign languages fosters precisely these capacities. (University of Michigan College of Literature, Science, and the Arts 2016)

When I am outside of this university context, it is jarring how differently multilingualism is viewed. In schools, the media, and the U.S. political sphere, speaking a language other than English (except in high school "foreign language" courses) is often seen as a detriment, a handicap, an obstacle to be overcome. Julie Nora and Jana Echevarria document how the low expectations that stem from this view can harm learners—the very learners whose skills would be so highly prized at my university. The authors offer strategies for building and expanding on the linguistic prowess of emerging multilingual learners. They demonstrate how such learners can not only survive but thrive in ambitious, content-rich instruction, provided that it is carried out appropriately.

I hope that this book has inspired you and others to continue to strive to provide the kind of education that enables emerging multilingual learners to see their linguistic abilities as an asset and that is sufficiently ambitious to prepare them for my university and other institutions of higher education. We look forward to welcoming them.

REFERENCES

Adger, C., and J. Locke. 2000. *Broadening the Base: School/Community Partnerships Serving Language Minority Students at Risk.* Santa Cruz, CA: Center for Research on Education, Diversity and Excellence.

Ardasheva, Y., and T. R. Tretter. 2012. "Perceptions and Use of Language Learning Strategies Among ESL Teachers and ELLs." TESOL Journal 3: 552–85. http://dx.doi.org/10.1002/tesj.33.

Au, K. H., and J. M. Mason. 1981. Social Organizational Factors in Learning to Read: The Balance of Rights Hypothesis. *Reading Research Quarterly* 17 (1), 115–152.

August, D., and T. Shanahan, eds. 2006. *Developing Literacy in Second-Language Learners: A Report of the National Literacy Panel on Language-Minority Children and Youth.* Mahwah, NJ: Lawrence Erlbaum Associates.

August, D., C. E. Snow, M. Carlo, C. P. Proctor, A. Rolla de San Francisco, and E. Duursma. 2006. "Literacy Development in Elementary School Second-Language Learners." *Topics in Language Disorders* 26 (4): 351–64.

Bauer, E. B. 2009. "Informed Additive Literacy Instruction for ELLs." *The Reading Teacher* 62 (5): 446–48.

Bialystok, E. 1988. "Levels of Bilingualism and Levels of Linguistic Awareness." *Developmental Psychology* 24 (4): 560–67. http://dx.doiorg/10.1037/0012-1649.24.4.560.

———. 1999. "Cognitive Complexity and Attentional Control in the Bilingual Mind." *Child Development* 70 (3): 636–644. doi: 10.1111/1467-8624.00046

———. 2001. *Bilingualism in Development: Language, Literacy and Cognition.* Cambridge, UK: Cambridge University Press.

Boser, U., M. Wilhelm, and R. Hanna. 2014. "The Power of the Pygmalion Effect." *Center for American Progress.* www.americanprogress.org/issues/education/report/2014/10/06/96806/the-power-of-the-pygmalion-effect/

Bottoms, G. 2007. "Treat All Students Like the 'Best' Students." *Educational Leadership* 64 (7): 30–37.

Brophy, J. E. 1983. "Research on the Self-Fulfilling Prophecy and Teacher Expectations." *Journal of Educational Psychology* 75 (5): 631–61.

Brouillette, L. 2012. "Advancing the Speaking and Listening Skills of K–2 English Language Learners Through Creative Drama." *TESOL Journal* (3): 138–45. http://dx.doi.org/10.1002/tesj.8.

Center for Research on the Educational Achievement and Teaching of English Language Learners. 2012. *Improving Educational Outcomes for English Learners in the Middle Grades: The CREATE Briefs Collection.* Washington, DC: Center for Applied Linguistics.

Cloud, N., F. Genesee, and E. Hamayan. 2009. *Literacy Instruction for English Language Learners.* Portsmouth, NH: Heinemann.

Cooper, H. M., and D. Y. Tom. 1984. "Teacher Expectation Research: A Review with Implications for Classroom Instruction." *Elementary School Journal* 85 (1): 76–89.

Crossley, S., P. McCarthy, M. Louwerse, and D. McNamara. 2007. "A Linguistic Analysis of Simplified and Authentic Texts." *The Modern Language Journal* 91 (1): 15–30.

Cummins, J. 1981. *Bilingualism and Minority Language Children.* Ontario: Ontario Institute for Studies in Education.

Dole, J., G. Duffy, L. Roehler, and P. D. Pearson. 1991. "Moving from the Old to the New: Research in Reading Comprehension Instruction." *Review of Educational Research* 61 (2): 239–64. http://dx.doi.org/10.3102/00346543061002239.

Dudley-Marling, C. and S. Michaels, eds. 2012. *High-Expectation Curricula: Helping All Students Succeed with Powerful Learning.* New York: Teachers College Press.

Duncan, A. 2014. "English Learners an Asset for Global, Multilingual Future." *Homeroom: The Official Blog of the U.S. Department of Education.* www .ed.gov/blog/2014/02english-learners-an-asset-for-global-multilingual-future/.

Echevarria, J., C. Richards-Tutor, V. Chinn, and P. Ratleff. 2011. "Did They Get It? The Role of Fidelity in Teaching English Learners." *Journal of Adolescent and Adult Literacy* 54 (6): 425–34.

Echevarria, J., C. Richards-Tutor, and M. Vogt. 2015. *RTI and English Learners: Using the SIOP Model, Second Edition.* Boston: Allyn and Bacon

Echevarria , J., and D. Short. 2010. Programs and Practices for Effective Sheltered Content Instruction. In *Improving Education for English Learners: Research-based Approaches*, edited by California Department of Education, 250–321. Sacramento, CA: CDE Press.

———. 2011. "The SIOP Model: A Professional Development Framework for a Comprehensive School-wide Intervention." Washington, DC: Center for Research on the Educational Achievement and Teaching of English Language Learners. www.cal.org/create/publications/briefs/index.html

Echevarria, J., D. Short, and K. Powers. 2006. "School Reform and Standards-Based Education: An Instructional Model for English Language Learners." *Journal of Educational Research* 99 (4): 195–210.

Echevarria, J., D. Short, and M. Vogt. 2008. *Implementing the SIOP® Model Through Effective Professional Development and Coaching.* Boston: Allyn & Bacon.

Echevarria, J., M. E. Vogt, and D. Short. 2017. *Making Content Comprehensible for English Learners: The SIOP® Model*, 5th ed. Boston: Allyn & Bacon.

Freeman, D., and Y. Freeman. 1988. *Sheltered English Instruction.* Washington, DC: U.S. Department of Education.

Garcia, E., B. Jensen, and K. Scribner. 2009. "The Demographic Imperative." *Educational Leadership* 66 (7): 8–13.

Garcia, G. E. 1991. "Factors Influencing the English Reading Performance of Spanish-Speaking Hispanic Children." *Reading Research Quarterly* 26 (4): 371–392.

Genesee, F., K. Lindholm-Leary, B. Saunders, and D. Christian. 2006. *Educating English Language Learners: A Synthesis of Research Evidence.* New York: Cambridge University Press.

Gersten, R., S. K. Baker, P. Collins, S. Linan-Thompson, R. Scarcella, and T. Shanahan. 2007. "Effective Literacy and English Language Instruction for English Learners in the Elementary Grades," Practice Guide Recommendation 5. What Works Clearinghouse. Accessed at: http://ies.ed.gov/ncee/wwc/PracticeGuide.aspx?sid=6.

Goldenberg, C. 2006. "Involving Parents of English Learners in Their Children's Schooling." *Instructional Leader* 29 (3), 1–2, 11–12.

Goldenberg, C., and R. Coleman. 2010. *Promoting Academic Achievement Among English Learners: A Guide to the Research*. Thousand Oaks, CA: Corwin.

Haycock, K. 2001. "Closing the Achievement Gap." *Educational Leadership* 58 (6): 6–11.

Hiebert, E. H., and M. L. Kamil. 2005. *Teaching and Learning Vocabulary: Bringing Research to Practice.* Mahwah, NJ: Erlbaum.

Jensen, E. 2008. *Brain-Based Learning: The New Paradigm of Learning*, 2d ed. Thousand Oaks, CA: Corwin Press.

Keene, E. 2012. *Talk About Understanding: Rethinking Classroom Talk to Enhance Understanding*. Portsmouth, NH: Heinemann.

Leinhardt, G., W. Bickel, and A. Pallay. 1982. "Unlabeled But Still Entitled: Toward More Effective Remediation." *Teachers College Record* 84 (2): 391–422.

Lesaux, N., and E. Geva. 2008. "Development of Literacy in Second-Language Learners." In *Developing Reading and Writing in Second-Language Learners: Lessons from the Report of the National Literacy Panel on Language-Minority Children and Youth*, edited by D. August and T. Shanahan. New York: Routledge, the Center for Applied Linguistics, and the International Reading Association.

Lyster, R. 2007. *Learning and Teaching Languages through Content: A Counterbalanced Approach*. Amsterdam: John Benjamins.

Marzano, R. 2010. "The Art and Science of Teaching/High Expectations for All." *Educational Leadership* 68 (1): 82–84.

Moll, L., R. Saez, and J. Dworin. 2001. "Exploring Biliteracy: Two Student Case Examples of Writing as a Social Practice." *The Elementary School Journal* 101 (4): 435–49.

National Center for Educational Evaluation and Regional Assistance. April 2014. "A Focused Look at Schools Receiving School Improvement Grants That Have Percentages of English Language Learner Students." *NCEE Evaluation Brief*. Washington DC: Institute of Education Sciences.

National Council for the Social Studies (NCSS). 2013. The College, Career, and Civic Life (C3) Framework for Social Studies State Standards: Guidance for Enhancing the Rigor of K–12 Civics, Economics, Geography, and History. Dimension 2: Geography 7.3–7.5: "Explain How Cultural and Environmental Characteristics Affect the Distribution and Movement of People, Goods and Ideas." Silver Spring, MD: NCSS. www.socialstudies.org/system/files/c3/C3-Framework-for-Social-Studies.pdf.

Neuman, S., T. Kaefer, and A. Pinkham. 2014. "Building Background Knowledge." *The Reading Teacher* 68 (2): 145–48.

Nora, J. 2013. "Language as the Lever for Elementary-Level English Language Learners." *Voices of Urban Education* (Vue). Annenberg Institute for School Reform, Summer.

Olsen, L. 2010. *Reparable Harm: Fulfilling the Unkept Promise of Educational Opportunity for California's Long Term English Learners*. Long Beach, CA: Californians Together.

Perkins-Gough, R. 2008. "Special Report/School Climate; Urban Parents' Views." *Educational Leadership* 66 (1): 89–91.

Rosenthal, R., and L. Jacobson. 1968. *Pygmalion in the Classroom*. New York: Holt, Rinehart, and Winston.

Ruiz, N. 2013. "It's Different with Second Language Learners: Learning From 40 Years of Research." In *High-Expectations Curricula: Helping All Students Succeed with Powerful Learning*, edited by C. Dudley-Marling and S. Michaels. New York: Teachers College Press, 145–161.

Santos, R. M., and M. M. Ostrosky. 2016. "Understanding the Impact of Language Differences on Classroom Behavior." Washington, D.C.: Head Start. http://eclkc.ohs.acf.hhs.gov/hslc/tta-system/teaching/Disabilities/Services%20to%20Children%20with%20Disabilities/Individualization/Understandingthe.htm.

Saunders, W., and C. Goldenberg. 2010. "Research to Guide English Language Development Instruction." In *Improving Education for English Learners: Research-Based Approaches*, edited by California Department of Education, 21–81. Sacramento: CA Department of Education.

Schmoker, M. 2007. "Reading, Writing and Thinking for All." *Educational Leadership* 64 (7): 63–66.

Short, D., and J. Echevarria. 2016. *Developing Academic Language with the SIOP Model*. Boston: Pearson Allyn & Bacon.

Short, D., J. Echevarría, and C. Richards-Tutor. 2011. "Research on Academic Literacy Development in Sheltered Instruction Classrooms." *Language Teaching Research* 15 (3): 363–80.

Short, D., C. Fidelman, and M. Louguit. 2012. "Developing Academic Language in English Language Learners Through Sheltered Instruction." *TESOL Quarterly* 46 (2), 334–361.

Short, D., and J. Himmel. 2013. "Moving Research on Sheltered Instruction into Curriculum and Professional Development Practice." Paper presented at the American Educational Research Association (AERA) Annual Meeting. April 28, 2013. San Francisco, CA.

Spitz, H. 1999. "Beleaguered Pygmalion: A History of the Controversy Over Claims That Teacher Expectancy Raises Intelligence." *Intelligence* 27 (3): 199–234.

Suarez-Orozco, C., M. Suarez-Orozco, and I. Todorova. 2008. *Learning a New Land: Immigrant Students in American Society*. Cambridge, MA: Harvard University Press.

University of Michigan College of Literature, Science, and the Arts. 2016. www.lsa.umich.edu/students/academicsrequirements/lsadegreesrequirements/languagerequirement.

Urbach, J., and J. Klingner. 2012. "The Storytelling Playground." In *High-Expectation Curricula: Helping All Students Succeed with Powerful Learning*, edited by C. Dudley-Marling and S. Michaels. New York: Teachers College Press.

Valdés, G. 2001. *Learning and Not Learning English: Latino Students in American Schools*. New York: Teachers College Press.

Vaughn, S., R. Gersten, and D. Chard. 2000. "The Underlying Message in LD Intervention Research: Findings from Research Syntheses." *Exceptional Children* 67 (1): 99–114. WIDA. 2014. www.wida.us.

OTHER FEATURED TITLES IN THE
NOT THIS, BUT THAT SERIES

Nell K. Duke and **Ellin Oliver Keene** help teachers examine common, ineffective classroom practices and replace them with ones supported by research and professional wisdom.

In each book a practicing educator and an education researcher identify an ineffective practice; summarize what the research suggests about why; and detail proven, research-based replacements that improve student learning.

Look to **Not This, But That** for doable solutions to issues such as classroom management, summer-reading loss, phonics and spelling instruction, and many more.

Visit Heinemann.com
for sample chapters and more information.

DEDICATED TO TEACHERS

To order by phone call **800.225.5800** or fax **877.231.6980**.

Prices subject to change without notice.